STILL GAME

STILL GAME

SCRIPTS: VOL 1

FORD KIERNAN &
GREG HEMPHILL

BLACK & WHITE PUBLISHING

First published 2004
by Black & White Publishing Ltd
99 Giles Street, Edinburgh EH6 6BZ

ISBN 1 84502 033 2

Copyright © Effingee Productions Ltd 2004

The right of Effingee Productions Ltd to be identified
as author of this work has been asserted
in accordance with the Copyright, Designs
and Patents Act 1988.

British Library Cataloguing in Publication Data:
A catalogue record for this book is available from
the British Library

Cover design: www.henrysteadman.com

Printed and bound by Bath Press

CONTENTS

FOREWORD FOR THE BOYS
by ROBBIE COLTRANE

I am delighted that 'the boys' (as they are affectionately known in our house), have done a book. Not least because it means that my son and I, who oft times slip into Victor and Jack mode, can at last get the words right. Especially whenever we're driven crazy by Pomposity, Aggravation and the sheer Stupidity that we all encounter in daily life.

Am I the only person who shouts, 'That's just pish, Jack!' when someone cuts me up in traffic? And who murmurs, 'That's enough, Isa!' when someone slopes into a Mega Gossip? I very much doubt it.

Like most Mega Fans of *Chewin the Fat*, I watched the first *Still Game* (caramel wafer in hand, natch), praying it would be as good. And lo! It was even better! The shows have always been terribly funny, as we know (classically, that Glasgow undercut that punishes any inclination we may have to fancy ourselves), but also beautifully observed. There's never any tendency to be phoney or forced and the pathos is always real – and often genuinely moving. The characters are believable, roundly drawn and stereotype-free. Just how on earth two such (relatively) young men came to inhabit a couple of loveable grave-dodgers with such panache and heart we will never know – but thank heavens they did. Enjoy.

1. FLITTIN'.

This is the very first *Still Game* episode. We used it to establish Jack and Victor's world. *Still Game*, in it's original form, was a one act play set in Victor's living room. The only people on stage were the two of us and Paul Riley. Isa was mentioned in passing as a nosy old bastard who lived across the landing. Obviously, by the time this episode was being written, we knew we would have to flesh out all the other characters and create an ensemble of players. For the keen eye, you will notice that the wigs and in general the overall look of 'Flittin'' are slightly different from the rest. It was filmed as a pilot a full 9 months before the other 5 episodes of the first series. It was directed by the producer, Colin Gilbert. While we waited for word on whether or not BBC Scotland would commission the series, the pilot

episode mysteriously turned up for sale down the Barras in Glasgow! (Dodgy buggers.)

When the series was commissioned, we went back and looked at this episode and tweaked and reshot about 7 minutes' worth with our present director, The Scouse Git, Michael Hines. If you are one of the lucky few people to have a Barras copy of the original pilot of *Still Game*, hang on to it. Keep it safe. In years to come, you may be able to sell it on ebay for 60, maybe even 70 pence. This is the episode that started the *Still Game* ball rolling and, as such, it will always be special to us. The pedants amongst you will notice that, dotted through the scripts, are scenes that never appeared in the screened episodes. Most of these were filmed but cut for a variety of reasons. They made the episode too long, they slowed the story or we made an arse of them and they didn't get any laughs. We've put them back in for you anyhow!

Ford and Greg

FLITTIN'.

1. EXT. JACK'S GARDEN. DAY.

WE SEE JACK IN HIS BACK GARDEN. HE TENDS TO HIS
BORDER WITH LOVING CARE. HIS GARDEN IS TINY BUT
IMMACULATE. HIS PRIDE AND JOY. FROM OVER THE FENCE
WE HEAR A RUMPUS. JACK LOOKS UP AND PEERS
DISCREETLY OVER THE FENCE. WE SEE HIS POV.

A MAGS HEANEY TYPE IS KNOCKING LUMPS OUT OF HER WEE
HUSBAND. SHE LOOKS UP TO SEE THE TOP HALF OF JACK'S
HEAD PEERING OVER.

MAGS: You wantin' some of what this useless bastart's gettin'?

JACK: Mornin'.

HE QUICKLY DUCKS
DOWN. A CIGARETTE
FROM THE OPPOSITE
GARDEN FLIES OVER
AND LANDS ON HIS
LAWN. JACK TUTS.
HE PICKS UP THE
CIGGIE BUTT AND
FLICKS IT BACK
OVER THE FENCE. HE
WIPES HIS HANDS
SMUGLY. AFTER A
PAUSE, AN ENTIRE
RUBBISH BAG IS
DUMPED ON HIS
HEAD. HE STANDS
THERE, COVERED IN
SHIT. THE DOORBELL
GOES.

2. EXT. HOUSE. DAY.

WE SEE VICTOR STANDING ON JACK'S DOORSTEP. JACK
OPENS THE DOOR, STILL COVERED IN TRASH.

VICTOR: Jesus! What the hell happened to you?

JACK: Shut up.

JACK GRABS HIS COAT FROM A PEG.

JACK: Clansman?

VICTOR: Aye. 'Mon.

3. EXT. OPEN GROUND. DAY.

WE SEE JACK AND VICTOR TRUDGING ACROSS THE
WILDERNESS BETWEEN THE HIGH FLATS.

VICTOR: You want tae see the council, get yer name doon and get tae hell
            ootae there.

JACK: I know. I'm sick of it.
            It's like living
            in the bastardin'
            Bronx.

VICTOR: Ye've got Mags
            Heaney on the one
            side and the Beverly
            Hillbillies on the
            other. They want tae
            drap a canister on that street and start again.

JACK: De ye mind when they built this place? Craiglang. The
            neighbourhood of the future.

VICTOR: Oh aye – Craiglang – modernity beckons . . .

JACK: Craiglang – the future is yours . . .

VICTOR: Craiglang . . .

BOTH: Shithole.

JACK: Here, I tell you what would be ideal . . .

VICTOR: Naw. For the umpteenth time, naw. Ye're no' movin' in wi' me!

JACK: How no'? Ye've goat space.

VICTOR: That's right. That's the way I like it – plenty of space.

JACK: I could stay in that big back room. Lovely.

VICTOR: What ye talkin' aboot? I keep ma . . . I use that fur eh . . . I'm never oot of that back room . . .

JACK: Right. Tell me – what's in that back room at the minute?

VICTOR: Eh? Um . . .Well, eh . . . the bed, sideboard . . .

JACK: Is that the bed and sideboard the Clenny took away last year?

VICTOR: Oh, aye. Um . . . Here, wait a minute, I've got the Matchbox racing circuit game set up for Wee Jamie.

JACK: Och, aye. Silly me . . . Wee Jamie . . . who just turned thirty. Lives in Johannesburg, merried, six year there.

VICTOR: He might come back. Things are rocky in Joburg, ye know?

JACK: Pish. That room's lying daein' heehaw!

VICTOR: Aye, mebbe so. But don't haud yer breath waitin' on an invite . . .

JACK: Oh, Jesus. Here they come. Don't look roon. They huvnae seen us yet.

VICTOR: Who?

JACK: Winston. And that boy
             – bloody Jersey Joe.

VICTOR: Aw, naw. He's gonnie
             railroad us intae gaun
             tae the lad's boaxin'
             match the night!

JACK: That'll be bloody right.
             We'll dae a runner.

VICTOR: Get a grip. Ye'll never outrun a minister's upright . . .We'll just tell
             'im straight. Piss aff. We're no' gaun . . .

JACK: Aye, aye. Listen, Winston, yer grandson couldnae fight sleep. Get it
             up ye. We're no' gaun.

VICTOR: Easy.

JACK: Done.

             WINSTON PULLS UP ON A BIKE WITH THE BOY RUNNING
             BEHIND HIM. WINSTON HAS A TOWEL UNDER HIS ARM.

WINSTON: Hello, lads. Comin' to the fight on Saturday?

BOTH: Oh, aye, wouldnae miss it. We'll be there.

VICTOR: Who's gein you a black eye the night, son?

WINSTON: Here, you. Wrap it. He's gonnie win the night, ain't that right, Joe,
             Boy?

             JOE NODS SHEEPISHLY. HE'S SKINNY AND DOESN'T
             RESEMBLE A BOXER.

JACK: Aye, well, Picasso, we'll be rootin' fur ye.

JOE: Picasso?

JACK: Aye. He spent a lot of time on the canvas as well.

             JACK AND VICTOR BOTH CREASE UP.

WINSTON: That's enough. Joe's comin' guid wi' ma coachin. Ye're definitely
             goin'?

VICTOR: Absolutely. Ye can coont on us. Dae we have tae go?

JACK: Aye, dae we huv tae?

WINSTON: Look. He's ma grandson, fur god's sake. The boy needs all the support he can get.

    WINSTON LOOKS TO JACK AND VICTOR. THEY STARE BLANKLY. THEY LOOK AT THE BOY. THEY DON'T WANT TO GO. AFTER AN AGE, JACK SIGHS.

BOTH: Right.

WINSTON: Right, Joe, on yer way. Two mair mile. I'll get you at the school in two hours!

    JOE JOGS OFF.

VICTOR: What's that under yer airm?

WINSTON: Towel. Sports centre. Every Tuesday. Senior Citizens' Splash Session.

VICTOR: Oh, aye?

WINSTON: Aye. Aqua Fitness. It's the way on. Cardiovascular star jumps, floating boards . . .

JACK: (nudging Victor) Pruned baws.

VICTOR: Pensioners pishin' in the water . . .

WINSTON: What would you know aboot it? The only exercise you two get is waggin' yer tongues, ya couple of auld wummin.

JACK: Ach, away ye go, Johnny Weissmuller.

VICTOR: Aye, piss off, Tarzan.

WINSTON: See ye the night.

BOTH: Aye.

4. EXT. NAVID'S SHOP. DAY.

> WINSTON IS WATCHING JOE HUMPHING BOXES OF SWEETS
> INTO NAVID'S SHOP. FOUR BOYS – THREE AGED ABOUT
> TWELVE AND ONE AROUND EIGHT – STAND UP AGAINST THE
> WALL, WATCHING.

NED 1:   Gie's a boax o' Curly Wurlies aff ye.

JOE: Nup.

NED 1:   Right. Revels, then . . .

JOE: Naw. Beat it.

WINSTON: Dinnae listen tae thae wee bastards! Right, youse, on yer way.

NED 2:   Naw.

WINSTON: C'mon. Take a tellin'.

NED 2:   Listen tae this auld rocket. Come ahead.

WINSTON: I'll set ma boy here oan ye.

JOE: Granda . . .

WINSTON: He's a boaxer.

NED 3:   I can see that. Takin'
            aw they boaxes intae
            the shop.

            THE NEDS LAUGH.

WINSTON: His hons are classified as dangerous weapons . . .

NED1:   Are your specs classified an aw, ya speccy auld bastard?

WINSTON: Right, Joe. See these wee tadgers aff . . .

JOE: Lads. 'Mon, noo. Let's wrap the pish and . . .

> THE EIGHT-YEAR-OLD HAS WORKED HIS WAY TO THE FRONT
> OF THE NEDS. RIGHT ON CUE, HE PUNCHES JOE IN THE
> BELLY. JOE IS DOUBLED OVER, BADLY WINDED. THE WEE BOY

DOES A VICTORY
SHUFFLE AND A FEW
QUICK JABS. THE
OTHER NEDS HOIST
HIM UP ON THEIR
SHOULDERS. HE
HOLDS HIS COAT
ALOFT LIKE IT'S A
BELT. THE NEDS RUN
OFF, HOWLING.

EIGHT-YEAR-OLD:
I'm Naseem! You're a pie! Eeeasy! Eeeasy!

JOE: He caught me aff guard, Granda!

WINSTON: Happens to the best of them, Joe, boy.

5. INT. SHOP. DAY.

WINSTON IS WALKING THE WINDED JOE INSIDE. NAVID
STANDS BEHIND THE COUNTER.

NAVID: What happened?

WINSTON: Gang o' neds jumped young Joe here. Wan got lucky and landed
one right in the breadbasket.

NAVID: (darting to the window) Is the van locked?

WINSTON: Thanks, Navid, fur yer concern. The van's emptied.

NAVID: Right. Well done, Joe.
Yer purse . . .

HE GIVES HIM A
LITRE-AND-A-HALF
BOTTLE OF DIET LILT.

NAVID: When's the big fight?

WINSTON: Saturday. Can you put
this up?

WINSTON HANDS NAVID A POSTER.

WINSTON: You gonnie make it, aye?

NAVID: Lemme just check my diary . . .

NAVID TURNS TO
MEENA. SHE SITS ON
A CRATE AT THE END
OF THE SHOP, HER
FACE IS OBSCURED
BY A NEWSPAPER.

NAVID: Meena. Fancy that?
Seeing the boy fight
on Saturday?

MEENA: (she speaks in her own dialect and the following translation appears:)
No chance – *Brookside* omnibus. I never miss it. Barry Grant comes
back this week and I missed it 'cause your sister was up.

NAVID: Aw, that's too bad. We've got a prior engagement.

MEENA: (chatters again)
Besides, our grand-
daughter could kick
that boy's arse.

6. INT. CLANSMAN. DAY.

WE SEE BOABBY, A FRAZZLED BARMAN, STANDING BEHIND THE
BAR TRYING TO READ A PAPER. A COUPLE OF WORKIES PROP
THE BAR UP. AULD TAM PROPS UP THE END OF THE BAR.

WORKIE: Two lager, mate.

TAM: 'Z'at youse breakin' fur lunch, boys? That'll be the community centre
nearly finished, eh?

WORKIE: Aye, just aboot.

TAM: I was in the buildin' trade masel' – many, many years. Then the old
            arthritis kicked in – boof. End of story. Look at that . . .

TAM HOLDS UP A
PAIR OF WIZENED
CLAWS. BOABBY
PLONKS DOWN A
PINT OF GUINNESS.

BOABBY: Wan ninety.

TAM: Wan ninety? Dear,
            oh dear. Is that what
            a Guiness is noo?
            Wan ninety?

TAM PUTS ON A GREAT SHOW, CLAWING ABOUT WITH HIS
BAD HANDS, TRYING TO GET TO HIS POCKET.

WORKIE: (resigned) I'll get that, mate.

TAM: Aw, lovely. I'll thank
            ye for that. Is that
            Club ye're smokin'?

THE SECOND
WORKIE OFFERS HIM
A FAG. TAM LIGHTS
IT, CRACKS HIS
KNUCKLES AND
WAGGLES HIS
FINGERS.

TAM: (to his pint) C'mere you . . .

BOABBY SPOTS JACK AND VICTOR ENTERING THE PUB.

BOABBY: Oh, here they are . . .
            Francie and Josie!

BOTH: Shut up, Dick!!!

THEY HIT THE BAR.

BOABBY: Fur the millionth time
            – it's Boabby!!!

EVERYONE SNIGGERS APART FROM BOABBY.

BOABBY:　　What would you like?

JACK:　　　What would we like, Victor?

VICTOR:　　What would we like? We would like to be warmer in here . . .

JACK:　　　. . . and for the décor to be more inviting . . .

VICTOR:　　. . . and to lose the smell of stale pish . . .

JACK:　　　. . . for you . . . to be an eighteen-year-old bird wi' big tits . . .

VICTOR:　　. . . to come in here and not want to kill wursels.

BOABBY:　　To drink.

BOTH:　　　Two lager.

JACK:　　　Victor would you mind getting this?

VICTOR:　　Of course, Jack!

JACK:　　　I must keep my change fur to tip the concierge in the lavatory who will no doubt offer me a fine selection of colognes from around the world . . .

VICTOR:　　Now – to lunch. What delights do you have on offer from your extensive and varied menu?

BOABBY:　　(flatly) Pies.

VICTOR:　　(with mock enthusiasm)　Ooooh, pies! D'ye hear that, Jack? They have pies!

JACK:　　　Oooh, pies – dandy. 'Cos we were gettin' sick of that lobster thermador.

VICTOR:　　When wis the last time we had a pie, Jack?

JACK:　　　Yesterday.

VICTOR: Och, well, pies it is then. Two pies as they come . . .

JACK: Cauld in the middle, roastin' roon the edge.

VICTOR: Irresistible.

JACK: Tam, are you havin' a wee pie and chips?

TAM: Oooh, a wee pie and chips? Aye, lovely.

JACK: (pointing at Victor's presented arse) Well, come back the morra and take it oot of there!

VICTOR: Ya poachin' bastart!

THEY FALL ABOUT. ISA, VICTOR'S NEIGHBOUR, GHOSTS IN AT THE BACK OF THEM, DRESSED IN BLACK.

ISA: Victor . . .

BOTH: Oaf, ya bastart. Jesus, Isa . . .

VICTOR: Didnae see you comin' in there.

ISA: I saw the perriyis comin' in there. Have ye forgot aboot the wake?

VICTOR: Who's wake?

ISA: Auld Mr Hannigan.

VICTOR: (turning away) Ach . . .

JACK: Old Man Hannigan? Yer next-door neighbour? Deid?

VICTOR: Aye.

JACK: How did ye no' say anything?

VICTOR: Ach, tae hell wi' im. Naebody on the landing has spoken to him in years – since he took a penalty kick at Isa's cat.

JACK: Aye, right enough. He was a prick.

VICTOR: Aye.

JACK: Here. Haud on. Will that be his flat up fur grabs?

ISA: I would say so. Nae family visits him . . .

JACK: That would dae me, that wee place . . . Here, Victor. We'll go tae the wake! That would gie us a chance to get a squatch at his flat!

VICTOR: (rolling his eyes) Christ, here we go again . . .

JACK: C'mon, think aboot it. Morning, Jack. Morning, Victor. That's me away intae ma hoose. That's me away intae mine . . . Cheerio! The two amigos.

ISA: The three amigos! I'm on the landing an' aw!

VICTOR: Mebbe ye're better where you are . . .

JACK: Aye, right enough.

THE MAGS HEANEY CHARACTER, WITH HUSBAND IN TOW, EXPLODES INTO THE BAR.

MAGS: I'm gaun fur a pish. Get them in.

JACK: You got a measuring tape in the hoose?

VICTOR: Aye. And ye wanting a lend of a black tie?

JACK: Aye. 'Mon.

JACK, VICTOR AND ISA EXIT HURRIEDLY. BOABBY ARRIVES WITH TWO HOT PIES.

BOABBY   Here! What aboot these pies?

TAM: Ahem . . .

BOABBY LOOKS ROUND TO SEE TAM PRESENTING THE TWO WIZENED CLAWS DESPERATELY. BOABBY GIVES OVER A PIE TO HIM.

7. INT. BUTCHER'S. DAY.

FROM THE BUTCHERS POV, WE SEE YOUNG JOE SHADOW-BOXING OUTSIDE THE SHOP. WE PAN ROUND TO SEE WINSTON COMING IN. HE WALKS UP TO COUNTER.

WINSTON: Right, Charlie, ma man, how's that lovely big wife of yours?

CHARLIE: She's laid up – food poisoning.

WINSTON: That's a good advert for ye . . .

CHARLIE: Eh?

WINSTON: Nuthin'. Now, here's what Ah'm after – a len' o' a chicken. For the boy tae chase, like oot the *Rocky* movie . . .

CHARLIE: Take a len' o' that . . .

HE PLUMPS A FROZEN CHICKEN DOWN.

CHARLIE: It's the only one he'll catch. He's rank rotten.

WINSTON: Shut yer hole. Typical. That's the trouble wi' folk roon here. Nae sense of community – of pullin' together. That boy represents hope. No' just for you. No' just for me. For the lot of us. For the

district. For the city. The world. It's exactly that attitude that's seen this country go wi'oot a champion for donkey's! It's no' what ye take oot – it's aw aboot what ye put in!

CHARLIE: Aye, I'm sorry, Winston. Put that in the boy. Beef 'im up . . .

           HE SLAPS DOWN A MASSIVE STEAK.

CHARLIE: Don't say I didnae dae ma bit.

WINSTON: Thank you.

           HE LEAVES, CHIN HIGH IN THE AIR.

8. EXT. BUTCHER'S. DAY.

JOE: I'm starvin', Granda.

WINSTON: Of course, son. Ye must be.

           WINSTON POCKETS THE STEAK.

WINSTON: C'mon we'll get ye a plate of chips at the Clansman.

9. INT. LANDING. DAY.

           JACK AND VICTOR EMERGE FROM VICTOR'S FLAT. VICTOR
           STRAIGHTENS JACK'S TIE. THEY RING HANNIGAN'S
           DOORBELL. VICTOR STUFFS A LITTLE NOTE PAD INTO HIS
           BREAST POCKET. HE NOTICES JACK IS HOLDING THE TAPE
           MEASURE.

VICTOR: Put that away, ya eejit!

JACK: Oh, right.

           THE DOOR IS
           OPENED AND
           VICTOR AND JACK
           TROOP IN. THEY
           WALK INTO THE
           LIVING ROOM,
           WHERE THE CORPSE
           IS LAID OUT.
           THERE'S A HANDFUL OF MOURNERS. IMMEDIATELY JACK IS
           PUZZLED.

JACK: Aaaao.

VICTOR LOOKS AT HIM QUIZZICALLY.

JACK: Mmmmmmn.

PEOPLE ARE BEGINNING TO NOTICE JACK'S ODD BEHAVIOUR.

JACK: (now on his haunches) Mmmmmmn.

VICTOR: (towering over him) What the bloody hell are you daein'?

JACK: This room's a lot weer than I imagined it would be.

VICTOR: (jabbing a finger at the coffin) Well, it will be a good deal bigger when
             THAT's no' here! Get up!

JACK: (getting up) That's what it is. Right. Scran.

THEY DISAPPEAR OUT OF SHOT. WE CUT TO SEE ISA
CHATTING TO THE PRIEST.

ISA: Terrible business, gaun suddenly like that . . .

PRIEST: Aye. And him wi' no family too . . .

BEHIND ISA AND THE
PRIEST, JACK AND
VICTOR SIDLE IN,
EACH CARRYING A
HEAPED PAPER
PLATE OF GRUB.
JACK OFFERS THE
END OF TAPE
MEASURE TO
VICTOR. HE GRABS
HOLD OF IT. THEY BOTH WALK BACKWARDS, EXITING SHOT
EITHER SIDE.

JACK: Fifteen feet.

VICTOR: Fifteen feet. Five yards.

AS VICTOR JOTS THIS DOWN, HE LETS GO HIS END. IT FLIES
OUT OF SHOT. WE HEAR IT RECOILING AT GREAT LASHING
SPEED.

JACK: Oowwwwwyabastart!!!

            VICTOR LOOKS UP.
            WE CUT TO SEE
            JACK.

JACK: (to a mourner)
            Ooowf. Have ye ever
            done that? They
            things are bloody
            lethal weapons . . . (SHAKING HIS HAND)

            VICTOR ARRIVES AND HURRIEDLY SHOULDERS JACK TO THE
            HALL.

JACK: (tutting) Shovin' . . .

            JACK AND VICTOR ARRIVE IN THE HALL. VICTOR SHOVES HIM
            INTO THE BATHROOM.

VICTOR: Get in there, ya hofwit.

JACK: Right. Bathroom suite . . .

VICTOR: One – avacada . . .

JACK: Shower . . .

VICTOR: One – seven kilowatt. Electric. Check the loo . . .

            JACK GOES OVER. HE FLUSHES THE LOO.

JACK: Guid order. Nice action.

VICTOR: Gie us a wee seat
            there . . . Oh. Very
            nice.

            VICTOR JOTS IN HIS
            NOTE PAD. THE
            TOILET DOOR
            OPENS. IT'S THE
            PRIEST.

PRIEST: (puzzled by what he sees) Beg pardon. Excuse me.

VICTOR: That's awright, Father. We're finished now.

CUT TO THE HALLWAY WHERE WE SEE JACK AND VICTOR.

VICTOR: C'mon. Let's collate wur notes.

JACK: Oh. There's yer bonus ball.

VICTOR: What?

JACK: A peephole intae the bargain!

VICTOR: Ooh, a peephole! I've aye fancied wan o them! Away outside and gie's a shot ae it.

JACK: Right!

JACK EXITS EXCITEDLY. VICTOR ADOPTS THE PEEPHOLE STANCE. WE HEAR JACK'S MUFFLED VOICE.

JACK: Can can ye see me?

VICTOR: Ye want tae gie's a chance tae get ma eye up tae the bloody hole? Oh, aye, there ye are there . . .

WE SEE VICTOR'S POV. JACK DANCES ABOUT.

JACK: (sidestepping to the peripheral) Can ye see me noo?

VICTOR: Aye.

JACK: (taking another step) Noo?

VICTOR: Just yer leg.

JACK: (leaping back into vision) Can ye see me noo? I'm a bogus gasman wi' fake ID. Let us in tae ransack yer hoose.

VICTOR: They'll be nae ransackin' the day. I'm up tae you. Fur this peephole's been yer undoin'. On yer way.

JACK: Open the door, auld pensioner!

VICTOR: Naw.

JACK: Open the door, I says!

VICTOR: I telt ye naw!

VOICE: Can you open the
             door please?

             VICTOR TURNS
             ROUND TO SEE THE
             COFFIN BEARERS
             ASSEMBLED IN THE
             HALLWAY READY
             FOR THE OFF.
             THERE'S AN
             EMBARRASSED SILENCE.

VICTOR: Absolutely.

             VICTOR OPENS THE DOOR. JACK IS MAKING SCARY FACES.
             HE SEES THE SCENE AND QUICKLY COMPOSES HIMSELF.
             THEY STAND ASIDE.

10. INT. PHONE BOX. DAY.

             WINSTON IS INSIDE, ON
             THE PHONE. WE CUT
             TO SEE JOE SKIPPING.
             HE JUMPS UP AND
             DOWN. THE ROPE
             PASSES IN FRONT OF
             HIS FACE.

JOE: Granda?

WINSTON: What is it, ma boy?

JOE: What aboot ma chips?

WINSTON: You'll get yer chips soon enough. Keep skippin'.

JOE: But, Granda . . .

WINSTON: Sssh! Hello, Lucy darlin'. It's Winston here. Aye. I'm needin' a robe
                fur ma grandson's fight oan Saturday. Right. That's enough. He's
                no' a big Jessie . . . Right. Smashin'.

                WINSTON PUTS THE PHONE DOWN.

WINSTON: (muttering to himself) Cheeky cow . . . Big Jessie . . .

                WINSTON LOOKS UP. HE SIGHS WITH RESIGNATION AT WHAT HE
                SEES. CUT TO JOE
                SKIPPING WITH TWO
                WEE LASSIES HOLDING
                THE ROPE PLAYGROUND
                STYLE. ANOTHER LASSIE
                IS PLAYING HOPSCOTCH
                AND ANOTHER PLAYS
                WALL-BALL. A CLASSIC
                'JESSIE' PICTURE
                POSTCARD.

11. EXT. SPARE GROUND. DAY.

JACK: He wis a good fella, Hannigan, weren't he?

VICTOR: He wis, aye.

JACK: De ye remember he went roon and put draught excluders on all the
                old pensioners' doors?

VICTOR: Aye. Free of charge. Practically built Isa's new kitchen fur nuthin'
                more than a cup of tea and a thank-you.

JACK: He just got on wi' himsel'. He didnae take any time aff ye. A real
                gentleman.

VICTOR: Aye.

                THEY ARRIVE AT A BUILDING. THERE'S A SIGN READING
                'HOUSING DEPARTMENT'.

JACK: Right. What have we to say tae these monkeys tae get the silly auld
                duffer's hoose aff him?

VICTOR: Here. De ye think we're being a wee bit premature? They've no' even
            planted him yet.

JACK: Ach! Pish!

VICTOR: Aye. Right. He who
            hings aboot getteth
            heehaw.

JACK: Right, Confucius.
            'Mon.

12. INT. HOUSING DEPARTMENT. DAY.

            JACK AND VICTOR SIDLE UP. THEY SIT AT A DESK IN A
            CUBICLE. A YOUNG LAD SITS DOWN.

LAD: Aw! Mr Jarvis! Mr McDade! How are you?

JACK: Oh, Jackie, boy! How's yer old da?

LAD: Still flying the pigeons.

JACK: Aw! Andy and his pigeons.

VICTOR: Pigeon daft, Auld Andy. Come rain, hail or snaw, ye'll always find
            him . . .

JACK: (leaning forward and
            interrupting) I'm
            needing a move.

LAD: Um. Oh. Right. Have
            you seen a place?

JACK: Yes. Next tae him. Up
            Osprey Heights.

LAD: Oh, right. Osprey Heights.

JACK: Auld Hannigan's house.

LAD: Oh, right. Dead, is he?

VICTOR: Aye. Well deid.

LAD: How long's the house been empty?

JACK: Hof an oor.

LAD: (stifling a laugh) Oh, right. Not wasting any time, then?

VICTOR: (grandly) He who hings aboot . . .

              JACK DIGS HIM IN THE RIBS TO SILENCE HIM.

JACK: So, am I gettin' it?

LAD: Well, usually, what would happen is I have to speak to the housing manager.

VICTOR: (coughing and producing a five-pound note) Why don't you speak to Rabbie Burns?

LAD: Actually, Mr MacDade, that's the Lord Islay.

VICTOR: (staring at the note) I always thought that wis Burns.

JACK: (producing two pound coins) Maybe we're not making wursels clear.

              JACK WAVES COINS UNDER THE BOY'S FACE. THE TWO OF THEM POSTURE WITH THE SEVEN POUNDS. THE BOY SMILES AND TAKES THE MONEY.

VICTOR: Money talks . . .

JACK: Bullshit walks . . .

              THE BOY TAKES THE MONEY AND PLACES IT IN A PLASTIC CHARITY BUBBLE.

JACK and VICTOR:
              Aw, shite.

VICTOR: C'mon, Jackie. Dae us a turn . . .

JACK: It's no' as if I'm jumpin' the queue. I'm freein' a nice pad up . . .

THE LAD SIGHS AND GOES TO A FILING CABINET BEHIND HIM.

JACK: If you would just let me move in wi' you, we wouldnae be havin' this
            hassle.

VICTOR: Look. Ye're no' movin' in wi' me. I'm no spending the last o' ma days
            watchin' you tannin' ma biscuit tin.

JACK: That tin's aye empty.

VICTOR: That's 'cos you've never got yer fat hons oot it.

LAD: Right.

HE LEANS IN CLOSER.

LAD: I'll get ma collar felt for doing this . . . but I can get ye the keys and
            you can sign the missives on Wednesday. Does that give ye time
            enough to organise a flittin'?

JACK: Ooh, now. That's fast.

VICTOR: (speaking over him) Aye.

JACK: Right, is that it?

LAD: Wednesday.

            THE LAD GETS UP
            AND LEAVES.
            VICTOR PICKS UP A
            PEN AND FISHES AT
            THE CHARITY
            BUBBLE.

VICTOR: Can that fiver be got?

JACK: Here, you!!!

            JACK PULLS OUT A
            PENKNIFE.

JACK: Try that . . .

13. INT. PUB. DAY.

WE SEE WINSTON'S PROTÉGÉ JOE IS WIRING INTO A PLATE
OF CHIPS. TAM WALKS PAST, APPROACHING THE BAR.

TAM: Boabby, there's me efter putting four-and-a-half quid in the cigarette
machine and got nothing.

BOABBY: (not even looking up from his paper) Ye cannae get fags oot a fruit
machine, Tam.

BOABBY LOOKS UP AT JOE.

BOABBY Here, Joe, is it Barry
Drummond you're
fightin' the night?

JOE: Aye.

BOABBY My Kelly Ann used
tae go wi' him. She
came ootae
Reflections wi' him
one night. Somebody called his maw a cow and he went mental.
He set about four bouncers. One of them lost an eye. Then the
polis turned up and he leathered the two of them. Ribs awe
smashed in and everything . . . he's an animal.

BOABBY REALISES
HE'S TERRIFYING JOE.

BOABBY: Mind you, he had a
drink in him – so
you'll probably be
awright.

BOABBY SAUNTERS
OFF. JOE IS SCUNNERED. HE PUSHES HIS CHIPS AWAY. TAM
LEANS IN AND REMOVES THE CHIPS.

TAM: Ye no' wantin' them, son?

WINSTON ENTERS.

WINSTON: That's me got yer dressin' gown fur the night, Joe, boy. Up ye get
tae we see ye in it.

JOE GETS UP AND PUTS ON HIS GOWN. HE DOES A BOXING
STEP AND SHADOWS.

WINSTON: It's no' new but it's a
          guid yin and it'll last ye
          a while . . .

          WE SEE IN BIG
          LETTERS ON THE
          BACK 'LUCY'S
          SAUNA'.

BOABBY: Here, son, I wouldnae
          wear that if I wis you.
          It's bad luck.

JOE: How?

BOABBY: Everyone that's worn that's been humped!

14. INT. JACK'S HOUSE. DAY.

          VICTOR ARRIVES AND ENTERS THE ALREADY OPEN DOOR.
          WE CUT TO INSIDE THE HOUSE. JACK IS FINISHING UP
          PACKING.

VICTOR: Awright, Jack, boy?

JACK: Where huv you been? I thought you were gonnie gie me a hon?

VICTOR: I wis waylaid. Auld Missus . . . eh . . . I wis helpin' Auld Missus . . .

JACK: Bookie's?

VICTOR: Aye, bookie's. Anyway, I'm here noo. What huv ye got left tae dae?

JACK: I've just tae gut oot that fridge.

          VICTOR GOES TO FRIDGE. HE OPENS IT. THERE'S A SOLITARY
          TIN OF TENNENTS IN IT. THERE'S A LAGER LOVELY ON THE
          SIDE, TO ILLUSTRATE HOW OLD IT IS.

VICTOR: Jesus, Jack! There's a lassie on this tin. This'll be well past its sell-
          by date.

JACK: Naw, naw. They didnae put sell-by dates on the tins back then.

VICTOR: So it'll be OK then?

JACK: Oh, aye.

VICTOR OPENS THE TIN AND POURS TWO GLASSES. HE COMES BACK INTO THE LIVING ROOM AND PUTS THE GLASSES ON A WEE TABLE.

VICTOR: So, is this yer whack, eh?

JACK: This? Aye – seven boxes, the bed, the suite and the sideboard.

VICTOR: Six boxes.

JACK: Eh?

VICTOR: That's a poly bag. That doesnae coont. Anyway, it's no' much is it?

JACK: That's tons. That's aw ma memories.

VICTOR: Awe yer memories in six lousy boxes? If ye ever write yer memoirs it'll be a pamphlet.

JACK: Here you.

VICTOR: Seventy-four years on the planet and that's aw ye've amassed?

VICTOR PICKS UP A HIDEOUS ORNAMENT.

VICTOR: And look at it – it's aw shite.

JACK SITS DOWN, LOOKING SAD.

VICTOR: 'Smatter wi ye?

JACK: Ah, ye're right. It is aw shite. Ye see I threw most of it oot – after Jean died. In fact, that ornament wis the only thing I kept. It was a weddin' present. She loved it.

VICTOR REPLACES THE ORNAMENT WITH RESPECT.

JACK: Efter I buried her, everywhere I looked I wis being reminded – the display cabinet, that whatnot thing that used tae sit in the corner, the wee trinkets that I hud by the fire . . . even that bloody twin-tub we hud in the kitchenette. I got shot of the lot of it. Start again. But I never quite got started again, did I? So that's how I've just got this . . .

THEY'RE BOTH QUIET FOR A SECOND.

VICTOR: Never mind, eh, Jack? Onwards and upwards.

VICTOR PASSES
JACK HIS GLASS OF
BEER. THEY
SILENTLY TOAST.
SIMULTANEOUSLY,
THEY BOTH SPRAY
THEIR BEER FROM
THEIR MOUTHS.

15. EXT. JACK'S HOUSE. DAY.

WINSTON AND JOE ARE USHERING A VERY ROPEY-LOOKING LUTON VAN TO PARK.

WINSTON: Back at that. Keep comin'. Back at that. Woah.

16. INT. JACK'S HOUSE. DAY.

JACK PEEKS OUT THE NETTING.

JACK: OK. Here we go.

VICTOR: Oh, is that yer van? Who's daein' it? Pickfords?

JACK: Awf. Pickfords! Away, fur Christ's sake. Winston's organised a couple of fellas that drink in the Clansman tae dae it – twenty quid and a pint.

VICTOR: Every penny's a prisoner . . .

JACK: What?

VICTOR: Nuthin'.

WINSTON: (shouting in at the door) Right. Get yer skates on. The boys are wi' me. And me and Joe's gonnie gie ye a hon. He could be daein' wi' the weight training!

JACK GRABS A KETTLE FROM A BOX AND HEADS TO THE KITCHEN. VICTOR FOLLOWS. THE MEN TROOP INTO THE LIVING ROOM.

17. INT. KITCHEN. DAY.

VICTOR: Ye'll no' be sorry tae see the back o' this place, eh?

JACK: Indeed I will not. Thae bastarts next door . . .

VICTOR: Aye, we'll get on fine, you and I next door tae one another.

JACK: Aye, you were right aboot me no' movin' in wi' you, but.

VICTOR: Aye. Here, what ye daein?

JACK: Just puttin' the kettle on fur half-time

JACK GOES OUT TO THE LIVING ROOM.

JACK: I'm just saying, will you boys be wantin' a cuppa fur half time?

JACK AND VICTOR ARE NOW STANDING IN AN EMPTY ROOM.

WINSTON: Hof-time? We're done!

WINSTON TAKES THE KETTLE FROM JACK.

JACK: Here, I've just remembered. That bastart next door's got ma garden shears. Here, Victor, away you nip next door and get them and I'll eh . . . finish . . . eh . . . just clean . . .

VICTOR: We'll go together.

18. EXT. JACK'S HOUSE. DAY.

> JACK AND VICTOR HEAD DOWN THE PATH, OUT THE GATE
> AND THROUGH MAGS'S GATE.

VICTOR: What the hell are ye wantin' wi' garden shears up the high flats
            anyway?

> AT THIS POINT, THEY ARE HALF-WAY UP MAGS'S PATH. A
> CHUNKY CERAMIC ASHTRAY FLIES THROUGH HER WINDOW
> AND LANDS ON THE LAWN.

JACK: Aye, guid point.

> THEY TURN ON THEIR HEELS AND HURRY DOWN THE PATH.
> THEY MEET WINSTON. JOE AND THE TWO LADS ARE HAVING
> DIFFICULTY PULLING DOWN THE VAN SHUTTER.

VICTOR: You wouldnae get that wi' Pickfords.

JACK: Shut up. Right, lads, is that you?

WINSTON: That's us . . .

VICTOR: Right, you know where ye're gaun noo? Osprey Heights. Along
            there, bang, bang, bang. Three blocks, turn right, eighteenth flair.

> THE BOYS JUMP IN THE VAN. IT DOESN'T START. THE MEN
> AND JOE PUSH IT. IT STARTS AND LUMBERS AWAY,
> BACKFIRING. THEY STAND AND WATCH IT TRUNDLE OFF.

JACK: It's a queer feeling,
            seein' aw yer life
            gaun aff in a van like
            that.

VICTOR: Off tae new horizons,
            Jack.

> HE PUTS AN ARM
> ROUND JACK.

WE HEAR A MUFFLED BACKFIRE. JACK AND VICTOR LOOK INTO
THE DISTANCE. THEY SEE THE VAN HAS STOPPED. SMOKE IS
BILLOWING FROM THE FRONT END. THE TWO OCCUPANTS
FLEE THE CABIN.
ANOTHER BANG IS
HEARD. THE VAN IS
ENGULFED IN FLAMES.

JACK: Clansman?

ALL: Aye, Clansman.

19. INT. VICTOR'S BEDROOM. NIGHT.

VICTOR IS SITTING UP IN BED WITH A WAR BOOK. HE LOOKS
FED UP. WE PULL BACK TO SEE JACK GETTING INTO BED
WITH TWO CUPS OF COCOA.

JACK: This is really awfy guid o' ye tae let us stay, Victor.

VICTOR: As soon as you get a bed, ye're oot on yer arse.

JACK: Understood. Ooh. That's smashin'. Is that an electric blanket ye've got?

VICTOR: Uh-huh.

JACK: What a heat. Roastin'.

VICTOR: Feet.

JACK: Sorry.

JACK TAKES A BISCUIT FROM A TIN BY THE BED. VICTOR
TAKES THE TIN. AS HE PUTS HIS HAND INSIDE . . .

JACK: We'll need tae get biscuits the morra.

VICTOR: Ya bastart!

HE HURLS THE EMPTY TIN TO THE SIDE.

CLOSING MUSIC AND CREDITS, THEN:

20. INT. RINGSIDE, COMMUNITY CENTRE. NIGHT.

> JACK, VICTOR AND WINSTON SHUFFLE PAST SOME SEATED
> SPECTATORS TO THEIR SEATS. THEY ARE CAUSING A
> DISTURBANCE. AS THEY ARE DOING THIS, OFF CAMERA, THE
> MC IS INTRODUCING JOE AND HIS OPPONENT. DURING THIS
> FIGHT, THE CAMERA NEVER LEAVES THE OLD MEN.

WINSTON: Quickly. It's about to start! C'mon, Joe, boy!

> WINSTON SETTLES
> BUT VICTOR AND
> JACK ARE TAKING
> THEIR TIME TO
> SETTLE, FOLDING
> SCARVES,
> REMOVING GLOVES,
> GETTING COATS OFF
> ETC. THE BELL
> GOES.

WINSTON: Leather him, Joe, ma boy!

> JACK AND VICTOR STILL HAVEN'T LOOKED UP. THEY ARE
> STILL SETTLING. AN ALMIGHTY THUMP IS HEARD. A CHEER
> GOES UP. JACK AND VICTOR FINALLY SETTLE. JUST AS
> WINSTON RISES UP.

WINSTON: C'mon.

JACK and VICTOR:
            Eh? What?

WINSTON: Blootered.

JACK and VICTOR:
            Aw . . . right . . .

> THEY ALL FILE OUT.

2. CAULD.

From time to time we hazard upon an idea that, we like to think, writes itself. This was one of those episodes and we wrote it extremely quickly – in about 4 days. Pensioners falling down, being neglected, stealing electricity. It was fairly straightforward and extremely good fun to write. It was also the episode where the character of Winston came into his own. Winston is the man who does what Jack and Victor are afraid to do, says what they are afraid to say and, in general, is the voice of the audience. Played with gusto by our good friend, the bloated roly-poly tubby guts Paul Riley. We are both great fans of slapstick comedy and this episode gave us a chance to do some.

At the press launch, we were asked continually whether or not *Still Game* and this episode in particular, was

dealing with heavy socio-political issues concerning old people in Scotland today. To which we answered, 'Pish.' Old people falling on their arses makes us laugh. Our favorite scene in this episode is when Jack and Victor have to make a phone call from manky Frankie's flat. Amidst the debris of fish and chip papers sits a stolen kiddie ride from Maryhill shopping precinct.

On a serious note, we did feel strongly that pensioners having to pay through the nose for electricity is a disgrace and, although we don't advocate breaking the law, we felt that Winston and all concerned were perfectly justified in doing so!

Ford and Greg

CAULD.

1. EXT. HIGH FLATS. DAY.

A GALE IS BLOWING. FROM THE WAY VICTOR IS DRESSED, WE CAN TELL IT IS SUB ZERO. HE IS TALKING TO ANOTHER OLD MAN.

VICTOR: What de ye make of this weather?

OLD MAN: Aye. The grun's aw slippy an aw. Nearly went on ma arse there.

VICTOR: (pointing to his shoes) It's a pair of these ye're wantin' – Permagrip soles. Timpson's – nineteen ninety-nine.

OLD MAN: Zat right?

VICTOR: Uh-huh. Ye've goat tae be careful at oor age.

VICTOR SLIPS ON THE ICE AND LANDS SQUARE ON HIS BACK.

VICTOR: Ugh. Ya bastard.

OLD MAN: C'mere. I'll gie ye a . . .

THE OLD MAN GOES UP IN THE AIR AS WELL AND LANDS FLAT ON HIS BACK. JACK APPROACHES.

JACK: Are youse awright?

OLD MAN: Mind yer feet, Jack. It's slippy.

JACK: It's a pair of these ye're wantin' – Permagrip soles. Timpson's – nineteen ninety-nine.

JACK FINISHES HIS SENTENCE AND GOES UP IN THE AIR AS WELL. THEY ALL LIE THERE, MOTIONLESS.

JACK: That boy at Timpson's is getting kicked squarely in the nuts.

VICTOR: Form a queue.

THEY HELP EACH OTHER UP. VICTOR PICKS UP JACK'S LOAF.

VICTOR: Who's this fur?

JACK: Wullie Napier. I feel bad tae. I said I'd pop up last Thursday. He's no' been keepin' well.

VICTOR: I'll come wi' ye.

JACK: Right–o.

JACK AND VICTOR EXIT FRAME LEFT. THE OLD MAN STILL LIES PROSTRATE. AFTER A FEW BEATS, JACK AND VICTOR RETURN AND HELP HIM UP. AS THEY DO SO, THEY ALL LOSE THEIR FOOTING AND COLLAPSE IN A HEAP.

2. INT. HIGH FLATS. DAY.

JACK AND VICTOR ARE AT THE LIFT. THE DOORS OPEN AND THEY GET IN. AT THE LAST MINUTE, WE SEE ISA RUNNING TOWARDS THE LIFT.

JACK: Quick, Victor, get in. I'm too cauld tae listen tae her pish this morning.

ISA: Haud the lift! Haud the lift!

VICTOR IS PRESSING THE CLOSE DOOR BUTTON FURIOUSLY.

VICTOR: Close, ya bastard.

THE DOOR BEGINS TO CLOSE. ISA WEDGES HER FOOT IN THE DOOR AND IT OPENS ONCE MORE.

JACK: Ooh, that was lucky, Isa.

ISA: (pressing for floor eighteen) Three for eighteen?

VICTOR: Naw. We're eight the day.

ISA: Oh, are ye gaun tae visit Wullie Napier?

VICTOR: That's right, Isa.

ISA: Lovely man. He's gone down hill awfy quick since he lost his wife.

JACK: Yes, Isa, that's right – downhill.

ISA: Is that you takin' him a wee broon loaf?

JACK: Certainly would appear so, Isa.

ISA: Oatmeal crust – very nice.

VICTOR HAS HAD ENOUGH.

VICTOR: Isa, for fu . . .

JACK: (stopping him) That's us – number eight.

THEY EXIT THE LIFT AND STAND AT WULLIE'S DOOR. THEY ARE ABOUT TO RING THE DOORBELL. THEY TURN ROUND TO SEE ISA PEERING OUT THE LIFT. SHE IS HOLDING THE DOOR OPEN BUTTON. THEY STARE HER OUT. SHE RELUCTANTLY LETS THE BUTTON GO. THE DOORS CLOSE.

JACK: Nosy auld bastard.

VICTOR GIVES THE ASCENDING LIFT THE FINGER. HE
NOTICES A MOTORCYCLE LYING IN BITS IN THE HALLWAY.

VICTOR: Look at this. It's like Annicker's Midden.

JACK: That's that lazy dirty
            bastard. I came doon
            tae see Wullie one
            time and there was
            an engine oot a
            Transit van lyin there
            pishin' its muck all
            o'er the flair.

VICTOR: Look at it – it's a heap
            of shite.

            JACK RINGS THE BELL

JACK: He's no' answering.

VICTOR: He'll be lying deid.

JACK: Shut up. I'll try again.

VICTOR: Aye, he'll be lyin'
            deid. Stiff and blue.
            Eyes staring.
            Pointing at you.
            'Wheeere huv ye
            been. Wheeere huv
            ye been . . . Where
            were you the night of
            the fifteenth, Jack??
            I've been deid since
            last Thursday! Yooou've kiiilt meee. Wuuur's ma
            broooown loaf???'

JACK: That's plenty. Ye're twistin' ma melon.

            JACK GOES TO SHOUT THROUGH THE LETTERBOX AND THE
            DOOR CREEPS OPEN. VICTOR TRIES THE LIGHT. IT DOESN'T
            WORK.

VICTOR: Away you in and scout. I'll wait here.

JACK: Aye, watch me. Come on.

THEY STEP OVER MAIL LYING ON THE FLOOR MOVING THROUGH THE HOUSE IN SEMI-DARKNESS. THEY ENTER THE LIVING ROOM. WE SEE FROM THEIR POV A HIGH-BACKED CHAIR. JACK AND VICTOR EXCHANGE A LOOK OF TREPIDATION. THEY APPROACH IT. TENSION BUILDS. THE CHAIR IS EMPTY.

WE CUT AS THEY SIGH WITH RELIEF. BEHIND THEM WE CAN NOW SEE WULLIE DEAD AND FROZEN, SITTING ON THE SOFA. HIS EYES ARE STARING, HE IS BLUE AND HE POINTS AT JACK.

JACK AND VICTOR TURN ROUND CASUALLY TO SEE HIM.

BOTH: Jesus!? Ya bastard!

JACK: (calling to Wullie) Wullie. Wullie . . . Wullie!

JACK: (to Victor) De ye think he's deid?

VICTOR: (sarcastically) Let's see, shall we?

WITH GREAT EFFORT, VICTOR REMOVES THE CUP FROM WULLIE'S GRASP. HE DINKS IT OFF WULLIE'S FOREHEAD. IT MAKES THE SOUND OF PORCELAIN ON PORCELAIN.

VICTOR: I'm no' Quincy, Jack, but I would say he's deid, yes.

JACK: Who do we call? The fuzz?

VICTOR: Naw, naw. Phone his boy.

JACK: Awf. I don't fancy that much. What a thing tae tell anybody. That yer faither's deid. There'll be tears.

VICTOR: What are ye talkin' aboot? He'll no' bother his arse. Look at the nick o' Wullie? When de ye think the boy wis up last?

JACK: Right enough. Make the call.

VICTOR: Naw, naw. I phoned Elsie Corrigan's boy when we found her deid.

JACK: So ye did. The corn beef sandwich? Lodged . . . terrible.

VICTOR: So come on. Get diallin'.

JACK: (picking up the phone) It's deid. He must have died. Then the phone got cut off because he didnae pay his bill because . . . he couldnae! Because he was . . . deid!

VICTOR: Very good Colombo. Let's go.

JACK: Where are we goin'?

VICTOR: We're gonnie ask manky Frankie if we can use his phone.

THEY TAKE A STEP BACK AND STAND SOLEMNLY.

VICTOR: Poor old bastard. He didnae deserve this.

JACK: Another good man down.

JACK SALUTES HIM.

VICTOR: Let's lay him oot. Bit of dignity.

THEY ATTEMPT TO LAY HIM DOWN. AS HIS BACK LIES DOWN, HIS FROZEN LEGS POP UP.

JACK: There ye are now, Wullie. We'll see wursels oot.

3. EXT. BARRAS. DAY.

WE SEE WINSTON BUYING A THREE-BAR ELECTRIC FIRE. HE POINTS TO ONE.

WINSTON: Gie us that one.

MAN: Right ye are.

WINSTON: And that one.

MAN: The baith of them?

WINSTON: That's what I said. The baith of them.

MAN: What de ye want the baith of them fur?

WINSTON: (like a mock inquisitor) What age are ye? Where de ye live? What size shoe are ye? Gimme the two fires, nosy!

4. INT. LANDING. DAY.

JACK AND VICTOR BUZZ FRANKIE'S DOOR.

FRANKIE: (answering the buzzer) What youse wanting?

JACK: Auld Wullie's died.

FRANKIE: Who's Wullie?

JACK: Yer next-door neighbour?

FRANKIE: And what?

JACK: His phone's aff. Can we use yours tae call his boy?

FRANKIE: Right.

5. INT. FRANKIE'S LIVING
ROOM. DAY.

FRANKIE, JACK AND VICTOR TROOP IN. THE PLACE IS A TIP. SIX TAXI TYRES ARE PILED UP. THE KITCHEN TABLE HAS A TAXI BONNET ON IT. THE FLOOR IS COVERED IN A SEA OF FISH AND CHIP WRAPPERS. ONE KID SITS ON THE LEDGE OF AN OPEN WINDOW, SMOKING. TWO KIDS SIT IN A CARTOON VAN EXACTLY LIKE THE ONES YOU SEE IN SHOPPING CENTRES. THEY ARE TAKING TURNS TO PLAY WITH THE STEERING WHEEL. IT IS MOTIONLESS.

FRANKIE: Phone's 'ere.

VICTOR: Are these fish and chip papers?

FRANKIE: Aye.

VICTOR: There must be a hunnert wrappers lyin' there. Ye must enjoy fish and chips.

FRANKIE: That's right.

VICTOR: Good.

JACK DIALS THE PHONE. FRANKIE'S GRUBBY FINGER CUTS IT OFF. HE POINTS TO A BOX THAT READS 'PAY FOR YOUR CALL. IT KEEPS THE BILL SMALL'.

FRANKIE: Pay fur yer call. It keeps the bill small.

JACK: Aye, I can read.

JACK MAKES A BIG JOB OF FISHING FOR A TWENTY PENCE. HE IS WITHOUT. HE TURNS TO VICTOR WHO IN TURN BEGINS TO FISH FOR A COIN

HIMSELF. HE PRODUCES A TWENTY PENCE AND GIVES IT TO
JACK. JACK PUTS IT IN THE BOX. FRANKIE LIFTS THE BOX.
HE SHAKES IT. IT'S THE ONLY COIN IN THE BOX. HE SHAKES
IT OUT AND HEADS OVER TO THE CARTOON CAR. HE PUTS
THE COIN IN A SLOT. THE CAR LIGHTS UP, PLAYS A TUNE
AND STARTS TO SHAKE.

JACK: That's eh . . . a rare thing. Where would you get a thing like that?

FRANKIE: Maryhill shoppin' centre.

JACK: Right. Smashin'.

VICTOR: Aye that is smashin'.

JACK: Hello. Michael, it's
            Jack – yer faither's
            pal. Eh? I'm fine,
            aye. Bit of a cauld
            last week. Quite the
            spell, intit? Eh? No,
            I'll no' get away noo.
            Mebbe a week next
            summer. Victor? Aye
            he's fine. Ye know
            Victor, eh? I'm across the landin' from him noo. Eh? No, I didnae
            go there in the end. Was Wullie tellin' ye? Aye . . .

VICTOR: (grabbing the phone) Yer da's deid. Ye better come up.

            VICTOR PUTS THE PHONE DOWN. ONE OF THE WEE BOYS
            STEPS UP TO VICTOR AND STARES AT HIM. VICTOR FISHES
            OUT ANOTHER COIN AND GIVES IT TO HIM.

6. INT. VICTOR'S HOUSE. DAY.

            JACK AND VICTOR STAND AT THE WINDOW. THEY BOTH HAVE
            OLD FIELD GLASSES AND ARE LOOKING OUT THE WINDOW.

            WE CUT TO SEE THEIR POV, THROUGH THE GLASSES. THEY
            ARE WATCHING THE ICE SPOT. WE SEE A MAN APPROACHING
            THE SPOT.

JACK: He's a cert.

VICTOR: Nup.

JACK: He's headin' right for it.

VICTOR: Naw. He'll miss it. 20p.

WE SEE THE MAN GO UP IN THE AIR AND LAND FLAT ON HIS BACK.

JACK: Ooh. Right on his arse. I'm 60p up.

VICTOR PASSES HIM THE TWENTY PENCE.
JACK SITS STARING AT THE FIRE WHICH IS OFF.

VICTOR: (heading to the kitchen) You wantin' a hot chocolate?

JACK: Aye. I'm freezin'. Here, Victor, I mean how are we supposed tae heat wursels wi' the pension they gie ye?

VICTOR: Millions the governments spent on advertising and leaflets tellin' what? 'Put oan a cardigan.'

JACK: I know. 'Stay warm this winter. Don't spend money of frivolous things – like food . . .'

VICTOR: 'Claes . . .'

JACK: 'or medicine. Scrimp and save on every penny ye can and gie it aw away to the electricity board.' I mean, tae hell wi' aw that, eh, Victor?

VICTOR: No.

JACK: You don't even know what I was gonnie say.

VICTOR: Aye, I dae. We're no' puttin' the fire oan.

JACK: Three bars. Wan oor.

VICTOR: Nup.

JACK: Two bars?

VICTOR RETURNS WITH HOT CHOCOLATE FROM THE
KITCHEN.

VICTOR: Have you any idea what that bastard burns?

JACK: What's the point in huvin' a fire if ye've never got it on?

VICTOR: Put the bulb on. That suggests warmth.

JACK: I'll tell ye what it suggests. It suggests ye're a dirty miserable bastard.

VICTOR: Away you intae yer oan house and get a heat.

JACK: I've no' got a fire. Ye know that.

VICTOR: And what is it you've got?

JACK: Electric fan heater.

VICTOR: And it's never on.

JACK: De ye blame me? It's a gutsy bastard. Nuthin' but an ornament. Aye, we're humped right enough. Do you know what's going to happen tae us?

VICTOR: What?

JACK: They're gonnie find us in the same nick as auld Wullie – these cups welded tae wur hons wi' frost. Two mair statistics. All because you wouldnae put yer fire oan.

VICTOR: Haud yer wheesht. The odds of us dying at the same time are astronomic. You'll go first.

JACK: Eh?

VICTOR: Aye. That pipe ye smoke. Bad circulation. Well before me, ye'll go. I'll eat ye. I'll walk ootae here a free man. Satiated.

JACK: You'll no' eat me.

VICTOR: De ye not think?

JACK: Naw. 'Cause ye're too tight tae burn the gas tae cook me.

VICTOR: I'll eat ye raw. I'm a survivor. In amongst ye. Nose first.

JACK: 'Zat yer patter? Before I die, I'll pretend tae die. And, when you sneak over wi' a mirror tae check I'm still breathin, (Jack makes a violent kicking motion) I'll snap baith yer skinny legs which'll be brittle wi' the cold by then. Then I'll pit yer fire oan. Three bars blazin'. And you'll lie there in a heap, watchin'. Face awe red wi' the heat. How'd ye like them apples?

VICTOR: (after a pause) Right. Wan bar, half an hour.

            JACK EXCITEDLY HEADS FOR THE ELECTRIC FIRE.

7. INT. PUB. DAY.

            JACK AND VICTOR ENTER THE PUB.

BOABBY: Oh, here they come – Abbott and Costello. You're puttin' the beef on, Jack.

JACK: Aye, I know. It's that wife o' yours. Every time I shag her, she makes me a sandwich.

            THE PUB FALLS ABOUT.

VICTOR: Aw, dear. There's Sammy Kane. He's pally wi' Wullie. Better tell him, eh? Sammy?

SAMMY: Aye?

JACK: Bit of bad news for you, I'm afraid, Sammy.

SAMMY: What is it?

VICTOR: Wullie's away. The cauld got 'im.

SAMMY: Awwww. That's Napier down. Who had Napier?

            THE BARMAN DOES A FIST OF VICTORY.

BOABBY: Yesss! Three to one – sixty quid.

TAM: (taking money from a coffee jar) Well done, Boabby boy. Good call.

JACK: Whit's gaun on here?

                WE SEE TAM GOING TO A BOARD. HE RUBS OUT NAPIER.

TAM: It's the hypothermia sweep. We're takin' bets on who's next tae go.

VICTOR: What!? Huv yez lost yer minds?

TAM: Dinnae come aw sanctimonious wi' us, Victor. It comes tae us aw.

JACK: Aye, but we're no' sittin' on a ticket waitin' fur people tae die.

VICTOR: Look at you sittin' there, Archie. How long did you work wi' Wullie? Thirty year was it?

JACK: (to the barman) And you, ya rat. That money should be gaun towards his funeral. You should aw be bloody ashamed of yourselves. Good neighbours, by Christ? Lookin' out for each other? What kind of community are we? Takin' bets of the death derby?

VICTOR: (quietly to Jack) Aff yer high horse – you left Wullie lyin' deid fur a fortnight.

                JACK SNUBS VICTOR AND TURNS THE TELLY UP.

NEWSREADER:

                Scots across the country are preparing for the coldest front since 1972. Temperatures are set to drop to as much as minus twelve in parts of the West of Scotland. Social Services are advising . . .

                THE BARMAN TURNS THE TELLY OFF. THERE IS A SOLEMN SILENCE, THEN A FLURRY OF BETTING ACTIVITY AROUND THE LEADER BOARD.

TAM: That's the odds down across the board. Wi' auld Eric the new favourite at 2–1 on account of they steel pins in his knee.

ERIC: (laughing) That'll be right. That's a wasted bet. I've got double glazin'!

8. INT. KITCHEN IN WINSTON'S FLAT. DAY.

> WINSTON IS DRESSED FOR THE SUMMER – TROUSERS TURNED UP, JESUS SANDALS, OPEN-NECKED SHORT-SLEEVED SHIRT WITH SWEAT PATCHES UNDER HIS OXTERS. THE BEACH BOYS BLARE ON THE RADIO. HE OPENS HIS FRIDGE AND ENJOYS THE COLD AIR. HE GETS SOME ICE FROM FREEZER. HE PLACES IT UNDER HIS OXTERS AND SIGHS HEAVILY. HE THEN PLINKS IT IN HIS DRINK. THE BELL GOES.

> WINSTON OPENS HIS DOOR TO JACK AND VICTOR.

WINSTON: Hey-ho.

JACK: Hello, Winston. Have you heard aboot this morbid sweep that Tam's runnin' doon at the Clansman?

WINSTON: That bastard.

JACK: Aye, he's a bastard.

WINSTON: He wouldnae gie me any mair that 3–1 on Jeannie Shaw.

VICTOR: No' you an' aw?

WINSTON: Lighten up. We're aw headin' that way. May as well make it interestin'.

VICTOR: Jesus, it's like the Belgian Congo in here.

WINSTON: Magic, intit?

JACK: Certainly is, aye. Wait till I take ma jaicket aff. Baltic oot there an' aw.

THEY PASS A THREE-BAR FIRE BLAZING IN THE HALL.

WINSTON: Mind yer legs there . . .

JACK AND VICTOR EXCHANGE A LOOK. JACK SPOTS AND
SILENTLY POINTS OUT TO VICTOR ANOTHER FIRE GOING AT
FULL TILT IN THE BEDROOM. THEY ARRIVE IN THE LIVING
ROOM WHERE ANOTHER TWO FIRES SIT SIDE BY SIDE IN THE
FIREPLACE.

VICTOR: Right, you, what's the story?

WINSTON: What do you mean?

VICTOR: Ye've got . . . three in
            the bedroom.

JACK: Three in the hallway.

VICTOR: Six in here – twelve
            bars of sweetness
            blaring away. What's
            going on?

WINSTON: Nup. I've got three going in the kitchen and another three in the
            cludgie an' all. Eighteen bars in total.

VICTOR: Right – spill it.

WINSTON: I cannae tell ye. I've sworn.

VICTOR: Get it telt.

WINSTON: I could tell ye but I'd incriminate mysel' – and by association, yersel'.

VICTOR: Winston.

WINSTON: Ye see, the thing is, Victor . . .

JACK: (bent double with the heat) Fur Christ's sake, gonnie tell us
            before we pass out?

WINSTON: Right, C'mere.

            WINSTON OPENS THE
            HALL CUPBOARD.

            HE SHOWS JACK AND
            VICTOR A STOPPED
            WHEEL.

WINSTON: Do you notice anything odd about the meter?

JACK: No, it's the same as mine.

WINSTON: Take a closer look.

VICTOR: The wheel isnae gaun roon.

WINSTON: For I have intervened and impeded the progress of said wheel. Observe. Watch what happens when I remove this.

THE WHEEL GOES SPINNING FURIOUSLY. THE MEN START BACK.

JACK: Jesus H. Christ Almighty. Look at the speed of that. It could cut diamonds.

VICTOR: It's like a sawmill. That wid have yer hon aff!

WINSTON: Terrifying, eh? Now if I was to leave that running, I would be potless and in the gutter by Thursday.

JACK: Ye would, aye.

WINSTON: However, with this wee device, I, my friends, am Winston – the King of Lecky.

BOTH: Unbelievable. Rare. Marvellous.

THEY ALL SIT IN THE LIVING ROOM.

WINSTON: Yes, indeedy. Help yersel' tae iced drinks, lads.

VICTOR: This is all very well but you know what this makes ye?

WINSTON: What would that be?

VICTOR: A thief. A rat thief.

WINSTON: Here we go.

JACK: Come on now, Victor.

VICTOR: Naw. That's how electricity's so dear. 'Cos the like of him is stealin' it. I'm no' bein' party tae it. Come on.

           VICTOR GOES TO LEAVE. HE NOTICES JACK STANDING SIDE BY SIDE WITH WINSTON.

JACK: No.

VICTOR: Eh?

JACK: Sorry, Victor. I'm wi' Winston. I'm wantin' a piece o' it.

VICTOR: Very well, Jack. Ye're a grown man and ye've made your decision. But consider this – ye're warm now but how will it be in a wee stony jail cell . . . wi' nuthin tae heat ye up but a warm boabie up yer erse?

           JACK RUNS THE SCENE THROUGH HIS MIND. AFTER A FEW MOMENTS, HE REJOINS VICTOR.

JACK: Victor's right, Winston. You're aff yer nut.

           THEY MAKE TO LEAVE.

WINSTON: Away youse two back tae yer ice boxes wi' yer wee principles intact.

VICTOR: And our arseholes an' all.

9. EXT. THE ICY SPOT. DAY.

WE SEE TWO KIDS SITTING ON A WALL. THEY ARE WATCHING A COUNCIL GUY GRITTING THE PATCH. AS HE WALKS BACKWARDS, HE GOES UP IN THE

AIR AND LANDS
CLEAN ON HIS BACK.
ONLOOKERS HOWL
WITH LAUGHTER.
THE MAN REMAINS
MOTIONLESS.

10. EXT. SPARE GROUND. DAY.

JACK: It would cut the face aff ye, wouldn't it?

VICTOR: Aye.

JACK: Smashin' over at Winston's, weren't it?

VICTOR: Aye. But crime doesnae pay.

JACK: Fair warms ye up, though, eh?

VICTOR: Aye.

11. INT. PUB. DAY.

A TWELVE-YEAR-OLD BOY IS SELLING PAPERS ROUND THE
TABLES.

TAM: (to the boy) Hello, Derek. How'z yer granfaither? Is he still laid up in
            bed?

BOY: Aye, he is.

TAM CHALKS THE
NAME JOHN BOYLE
FROM 3–1 TO 2–1.

TAM: That's a shame.

BOY: But my mammy
            bought him an
            electric blanket. Doctor says he should be up and aboot in a
            couple of days.

TAM: Oh, good.

TAM CHALKS HIM OUT TO 6–1.

12. INT. CORNER SHOP. DAY.

JACK AND VICTOR STEP IN.

JACK: Hello, Navid. Two ounce o' Drum, if you please.

VICTOR: How ye keepin', Navid?

NAVID: No' bad. My boy wrote aff ma car last night.

VICTOR: Wee bastard.

NAVID: Aye, well, I'm takin' next week aff. That wee fanny can get up at six o'clock and take the rolls in.

JACK: Awfy warm in here, Navid.

NAVID: Aye. Scratch card?

JACK: Aye. Two Lucky Donkeys, as per.

NAVID: Two Donkeys . . .

THEY BACK OUT OF THE SHOP, EYEING NAVID SUSPICIOUSLY. NAVID JUST STARES BLANKLY AT THEM.

13. EXT. SHOP. DAY.

JACK AND VICTOR SILENTLY SCRATCH AWAY AT THEIR CARDS.

BOTH: Op. Ooooop. Bastard.

THEY THROW AWAY THE CARDS IN TANDEM.

14. EXT. BOOKIE'S. DAY.

> JACK AND VICTOR BATTLE THE WIND ON THEIR WAY TO THE BOOKIE'S.

JACK: De ye think he was at it?

VICTOR: Aye. He had a look in his eye.

JACK: Aye, he did. A sorta 'I'm gettin' free lecky and youse two are a couple of wankers fur payin' oot' look . . .

15. INT. BOOKIE'S. DAY.

> JACK AND VICTOR STEP IN. THEY ARE WRAPPED UP BUT EVERYONE ELSE IS DRESSED DOWN. THE PLACE IS LIKE AN OVEN. EVERYONE FANS THEMSELVES WITH BETTING SLIPS AND RACING FORMS.

MAN: Close the door. Ye're lettin' the cauld in!!!

VICTOR: Sorry.

> VICTOR CLOSES THE DOOR. JACK AND VICTOR LOOK PUZZLED. THEY MAKE THEIR WAY TO THE COUNTER, SLOWLY PASSING SILENT CUSTOMERS LIKE A SCENE FROM THE BIRDS.

BOTH: Jackie. Frank. Stevie. Wullie. Cammie.

> THEY STAND AT THE COUNTER.

JACK: (writing as he speaks) 3.30 Chepstow – Captain Howdy.

VICTOR: (looking round) Each way.

JACK: Each way. Warm in here, Tracy.

TRACY: (suspicious) Think so? Stevie.

STEVIE: Aye.

TRACY: Do you feel it warm in here?

STEVIE: Not overly, no.

VICTOR: C'mon. I'm gettin' the
             fear.

             THEY BEGIN TO
             BACK AWAY,
             TOWARDS THE EXIT.

BOTH: Cammie. Wullie.
             Stevie. Frank. Jackie.

             AS THEY EXIT, ALL EYES ARE ON THEM.

16. INT. CAFE. DAY.

             JACK AND VICTOR SIT IN THE RENDEZVOUS CAFÉ. THEY SIP
             BOVRIL.

JACK: Everyone's at it, Victor. They're all stealin' leccy.

VICTOR: Ah know. Doesnae make it right, but.

             THEY HEAR WINSTON'S VOICE AS HE EMERGES FROM THE
             BACK ROOM.

WINSTON: That's you now. Get the heatin' up!

VICTOR: Winston! What are you daein back there?

WINSTON: Serving the community.

VICTOR: Mair theivin', ya daftie.

WINSTON: You're the dafties here.

VICTOR: How?

             WINSTON SITS
             DOWN.

WINSTON: We've worked aw
             wur days. For what?
             Tae sit freezin',

wonderin' if the phone's gonnie go, feart tae burn the fire – waitin' on the reaper. A baw hair away fae eatin' dug food.

VICTOR: It's no' that bad.

WINSTON: It is that bad. The government want us tae die. We're obliged tae die. Tony Blair, every morning, 'Here, you, ma wee government lacky, how many auld bastards died last night? 1500. Smashin'. That'll free up some housing stock.' Do you know what pensioners are? Lepers. We take, take, take. And we gie nuthin' back. And they hate us fur it. They cannae wait tae bury us.

JACK: Aye.

WINSTON: Do youse two silly bastards know that ye're even money in the hypothermia sweep?

VICTOR: Eh?

WINSTON: Aye. 'Cause ye'll no' take free leccy. Even money. Ye should be ashamed of yersels. Do you know who else is even money?

VICTOR: Who?

WINSTON: Auld Peter.

JACK: The jakey?

WINSTON: That's right. Drank his hoose, wife, weans, dug, the lot. Lives outside. Even money – same as youse.

JACK: I'm no' havin' ma odds the same as that smelly bastard. That's a brass neck. I'm in.

VICTOR: What the hell are ye sayin'?

JACK: I'm in. I gie up. Free leccy. C'mon, Winston. Let's get it rigged up.

THEY LEAVE. VICTOR FOLLOWS THEM OUT.

VICTOR: Think aboot this, Jack!

JACK: I huv thought aboot it! I dunno about you, Victor, but I quite like the mad notion of surviving the winter.

WINSTON: That's it, Jack. Get him telt.

VICTOR: You shut yer hole, ya footpad! Ye're draggin' him doon tae yer ain level!

JACK: He's draggin' me naewhere! I've made ma decision. I'll see ye later on.

VICTOR: Ye'll no' see me later on. I don't hing aboot wi' the underworld.

JACK: Arsehole.

VICTOR: Prick.

JACK AND WINSTON LEAVE. VICTOR STANDS ALONE. HIS HAT BLOWS OFF HIS HEAD AND LANDS IN A PUDDLE. HE CUTS A LONELY FIGURE.

17. INT. CHURCH. DAY.

JACK AND WINSTON SIT TOGETHER MOURNFULLY AT THE FUNERAL OF WULLIE NAPIER. WE HEAR ORGAN MUSIC.

JACK: Bloody shame, right enough.

WINSTON: Aye. What a way tae end up. An ice lolly. Daft auld bastard.

JACK: Haw, you. Show a little respect.

VICTOR APPEARS. HE NUDGES THE MEN UP TO MAKE A SPACE.

VICTOR: Look at youse two, eh? Thick as thieves. What are ye up tae? Plannin' yer next heist? The church silver, is it?

WINSTON: How's life up at Frosty Towers? Adequate?

VICTOR: Ample, yes. Thank you.

VICTOR REMOVES HIS SCARF.

WINSTON: Feelin' it quite warm in here, are you, Victor?

VICTOR: Uh-huh.

WINSTON: You might be interested to learn that Father Graham has availed himself of my services.

VICTOR: Pish. Don't you be tellin' lies in a house of God.

WINSTON: I can assure you it's the truth. Yes, it would appear that the good Lord himself likes it toasty.

VICTOR SCANS THE ROOM. THERE ARE A COUPLE OF AULD YINS FANNING THEMSELVES WITH HATS.

VICTOR: You're at it.

THE PRIEST IS NOW LEADING THE FUNERAL PROCESSION OUT THE CHURCH.

WINSTON: (catching the priest's eye) Father. Nice and warm in here today . . .

THE PRIEST MIMES HIS GRATITUDE FOR THE HEAT. HE RUBS HIS ARMS TOASTILY. VICTOR IS SHATTERED.

18. INT. VICTOR'S FLAT. DAY

> VICTOR IS SLEEPING ON THE SOFA. HE LOOKS FROZEN. HE
> SPORTS A WOOLLY HAT, SCARF AND A PAIR OF MITTENS.
> JACK ENTERS.

JACK: (whispering) Victor.

VICTOR: Jack. What time is it?

JACK: Time you got a bloody heat in ye. Ye're freezing. Feel yer face.

VICTOR: I'm alright.

> WINSTON APPEARS.
> HE AND JACK LEAD
> VICTOR TO A
> MIRROR. THEY LIFT
> HIS ARMS. HE SEES
> HIS PATHETIC
> IMAGE.

VICTOR: Hook me up.

JACK: 'Ere ye are.

> WE NOW GET A MONTAGE SEQUENCE OF WINSTON OPENING
> HIS BRIEFCASE AND ASSEMBLING HIS POWER DRILL,
> SCREWDRIVER AND A CRISS-CROSS STOOL.

WINSTON: (presenting his drill) Let's go tae work.

19. INT. LIVING ROOM. DAY.

> JACK AND VICTOR SIT IN THE LIVING ROOM. BETWEEN THEM,
> IN THE HALL, WE SEE WINSTON ATOP THE STOOL BEAVERING
> AWAY AT THE LECCY METER.

JACK: Ye're dain' the right thing, ye know.

VICTOR: I know. I'm a daft auld bugger.

JACK: I wasnae gonnie tell ye this . . .

VICTOR: What?

JACK: I hud a dream about
            Wullie the other
            night.

VICTOR: What happened?

JACK: He had a shroud
            roon 'im. His coupon
            wis blue like iced water. Eyes yella.

VICTOR: He always hud yella eyes, didn't he?

JACK: Aye. Aw the drinkin' he'd done.

VICTOR: So . . .

JACK: He took me by the hon. His hon wis freezin'. He led me up these
            beautiful stairs. Wi' nae bannisters. I'm lookin' side tae side and I
            cannae see the end of the stairs. Eventually we get to the top. But
            I'm no' puffed oot. Wullie points. Like he wis that day when we found
            him . . . He points at a coffin. Wi' the lid doon. Not a new one. An
            auld one. Musty. Like it'd been dug up.

VICTOR: Exhumed.

JACK: Aye. Exhumed. I'm
            feart. But he grips
            me tighter. He's
            pullin' me ower. I'm
            sayin' tae him,
            'Who's in the coffin?
            Who's in the coffin?'
            But he cannae
            answer me. 'Cause
            he's got nae mooth.
            I'm touchin' where his mooth should be. But it's awe smooth. Like
            porcelain. We're at the coffin now. And I cannae move. I'm lookin'
            doon at it. And Wullie's opening it. And that's when I see. Right
            there, in the coffin, starin' right at me – the body of . . .

            AT THIS MOMENT, THERE'S A LOUD EXPLOSION. WINSTON IS
            THROWN BACK AND GOES OUT OF VISION PAST THE
            DOORWAY. HE THEN WALKS BACK INTO THE DOORWAY.

WINSTON: (slightly fazed, hair slightly unkempt) That's all right. That happens sometimes.

WINSTON HEADS BACK TO WORK.

VICTOR: Jesus! I just aboot shat masel'.

JACK: Are you done yet? C'mon, fur God's sake.

WINSTON: Just a wee . . . There ye are! Welcome to FEC. The Free Electricity Club. Right! Gather roon the fire for the ceremonial turning on of the fire.

THEY ALL GATHER ROUND.

JACK: How do you feel? Feels pretty good, eh?

VICTOR: It does that. Aye.

JACK: Well. Turn it on.

VICTOR: Eh. Aye. Right.

VICTOR TURNS ON THE FIRE. HE STANDS BACK UP AGAIN. HE SMILES. THE OTHER TWO LOOK PUZZLED.

WINSTON: One bar?

VICTOR: One bar's plenty.

JACK: It's gratis, Victor! Get the three bars on!

VICTOR RELUCTANTLY BENDS DOWN TO PUT ON THE THREE BARS. WE CUT TO SEE THE EXTERIOR TOWER BLOCK. AS VICTOR SPEAKS, THE ENTIRE BLOCK EXCEPT VICTOR'S HOUSE IS PLUNGED INTO DARKNESS.

VICTOR: (voice over) There we are. That's rare. I cannae mind the last time
            I had the three bars on.

WINSTON: (voice over) Aye. Ye can smell the stoor burnin'.

JACK: Right, I'm gonnie put the free kettle on.

            THERE ARE A COUPLE OF BEATS. WE HEAR A CLICK. THE
            NEIGHBOURING TOWER BLOCK IS PLUNGED INTO DARKNESS.

JACK: Free hot water. Free tea.

VICTOR: What else can we turn on?

WINSTON: Ye're gettin' the hang of it noo. The telly!

            AS WE HEAR THE TELLY CLICKING ON, THE WHOLE SCHEME
            IS PLUNGED INTO DARKNESS, BAR THE LIGHT IN VICTOR'S
            HOUSE.

VICTOR: I suppose that's the beauty of it. There are that many people in this
            scheme ye'll never know who's stealin' it!

CLOSING MUSIC AND CREDITS, THEN:

            JACK AND VICTOR SIT ON A CONCRETE BENCH NEAR THE ICY
            PATCH OUTSIDE THE FLATS.

VICTOR: It's nice tae get a bit of cauld air roon aboot ye. Gies ye a break
            from sittin' in that oven of a flat.

JACK: Aye. Oop. Here
            comes Mary Stewart.

VICTOR: Auld Wiggy.

JACK: It's no' a wig. Ye're
            aye sayin' it's a wig.

VICTOR: She's baldy! Course
            it's a wig. It's like a
            hat!

JACK: It's no' a wig.

MARY STEWART HITS THE ICY SPOT. SHE IS THROWN UP IN
THE AIR AND LANDS ON HER BACK. HER WIG FLIES OFF.

JACK: Jeezo. It is a wig right enough.

MARY DUSTS HERSELF DOWN AND PLONKS THE WIG ON LIKE
A HAT.

VICTOR: Here. Ye never did tell me who wis in the coffin?

JACK: What?

VICTOR: That dream ye hud wi' Wullie.

JACK: Oh, aye. Aye, well, he opened the coffin and there it was – the body
            of Jack Lord. Weird that. Eh?

VICTOR: Who's Jack Lord?

JACK: Cop. Hawaii 5–0.

VICTOR: Is he deid?

JACK: I dunno.

3. COURTIN'.

This episode grew out of a simple plot line – Jack and Victor go out on a date. During a transmission run of a series people always stop you to tell you what they think of a given episode. The feedback on this one was that it was a lot of folks' favourite. In some ways, it embodies everything that *Still Game* is about. Sad in bits, funny in others. Jack reminisces about the loss of his wife and Victor's date is as ugly as sin. The script detail for Edith is fairly minimal. She is an ugly woman. This is one of those instances, where the make up and wardrobe people as well as the performance of Maureen Carr combine to make Edith's entrance off the bus the standout moment in this episode.

We always find it enjoyable to put Winston through the wringer and this episode sees him being barred from

the Clansman by Boabby, played by Gavin Mitchell. Gavin was the original Winston in two sketches put out in a TV programme called *Pulp Video* in 1996. The following summer, having written the stage show, we asked Gavin to reprise the role. Unfortunately he was unavail-able and we had to settle for sloppy seconds super-sub Paul Riley. By the time the show came to television, Paul had made the part his own and so we set about writing a character for Gavin. Boabby is one of our favourite characters and over the three series transmitted so far you will notice his part has grown and grown. We love Boabby!

Ford and Greg

COURTIN'.

1. EXT. CLANSMAN. DAY.

BOABBY OPENS THE DOOR AND POINTS TO THE OUTSIDE.
WINSTON WALKS OUT.

BOABBY: Out. Ye're barred.

WINSTON: Stick yer pub up yer
           arse. How long fur?

BOABBY: Indefinately.

2. EXT. TOWN CENTRE. DAY.

VICTOR: What huv you still tae dae?

JACK: (reading note) I've tae get a key cut, two bulbs for the hall. Bayonet
            – no' screw-in – a battery for the doorbell, a bottle of Windolene,
            some dusters and a belt fur the hoover. (he turns the note over) Get
            a pint.

VICTOR: Right. Which of those things will we dae first?

3. INT. BAR. DAY.

WE CUT TO SEE
JACK AND VICTOR
ENJOYING A HALF
AND HALF IN AN
IRISH THEME BAR.
RIVERDANCE MUSIC
IS PIPED IN.

VICTOR: What wis the name of
            this shop again?

JACK: I dunno. Barry O'Themes.

VICTOR: 'Kin shitehole.

BARMAN: (delivering two pies) There ye go, gentlemen. Top o' the mornin' and
            the luck o' the Irish!

JACK: What part of Ireland
            are you fae?

BARMAN: (in a strong Glasgow
            accent) Springburn.

JACK: What's in the bag?

VICTOR: Auld claes – fur the
            charity shop.

JACK: The one in the precinct?

VICTOR: Aye.

JACK: Fine. Good.

VICTOR: What's the matter wi' your face?

JACK: Nuthin'.

4. EXT. CHARITY SHOP. DAY.

VICTOR: I hope that big honey's on – wi' the tits.

JACK: Hey, hey, hey.

VICTOR: What?

JACK: Wrap that – the tits.

VICTOR: Right-o, Gentleman Jack. Ye comin' in?

JACK: Nup. I'll wait here.

VICTOR: 'Smatter wi' ye? Ye went aff tits?

JACK: Shut up. I'll staun here and smoke ma pipe.

VICTOR: Get in. Are ye daft?

            THEY ENTER

5. INT. CHARITY SHOP. DAY.

            VICTOR AND JACK APPROACH THE COUNTER. JACK LOOKS
            SHY. AN ATTRACTIVE OLDER WOMAN IS AT THE COUNTER.

VICTOR: Hello, ma darlin'. De ye remember us?

WOMAN: Um. I think so . . .

VICTOR: The two debonair patter merchants fae Craiglang?

WOMAN: Aw, yes. How could I forget? What would you like to give me?

VICTOR: A night on the town, cosy meal, bottle of wine, dance till two . . .

JACK: Meal . . . wine and dancin'.

WOMAN: I meant in the bag!

VICTOR: That's the mystery,
            sweetheart. What's
            in the . . .

JACK: Auld claes.

            VICTOR LEADS JACK
            BY THE ELBOW.

VICTOR: What's the score wi' you?

JACK: Eh?

VICTOR: Where's the auld silver tongue? I'm battin' them up for ye and you're
            sleepin'! (he mimics Jack) 'Auld claes!' Where's the banter? The old
            double act?

JACK: I cannae be arsed. Leave her alane.

VICTOR: Leave her alane? (Victor twigs) Op. You fancy her.

JACK: I do not.

VICTOR: Aye, ye dae. Ye're takin' a beamer!

JACK: No, I'm no'. It's just too warm in here.

VICTOR: Ask her oot. She's lovely.

JACK: Don't be ridiculous.

VICTOR: Nuthin' ridiculous aboot it. Ask her oot fur a wee meal or somethin'.

JACK: De ye think?

VICTOR: Aye. 'Mon.

JACK AND VICTOR SIDLE OVER TO THE DESK. JACK LOOKS
PALE AND SCARED. THE SHOPKEEPER LOOKS BEMUSED.

VICTOR: Forgive me, sweetheart, we don't even know yer name.

WOMAN: Barbara.

VICTOR: Barbara. Lovely. My
friend has something
he'd like to ask you.

WOMAN: Oh.

WE CUT TO SEE
JACK ROOTED TO
THE SPOT. WE CUT
TO BARBARA IN
EXPECTATION. BACK TO JACK. TO BARBARA. TO VICTOR. TO
JACK. HE TURNS AND RUNS LIKE A CHILD, KNOCKING OVER A
RAIL. HE EXITS THE SHOP. VICTOR EXITS IN HOT PURSUIT.

6. EXT. SPARE GROUND. DAY.

VICTOR IS LOOKING ABOUT. JACK IS NOWHERE TO BE SEEN.
VICTOR SPOTS WINSTON WHO IS HANGING ABOUT WITH A
BUNCH OF KIDS DRINKING ALCOPOPS.

VICTOR: Here, Winston, ye huvnae seen Jack, huv ye?

WINSTON: Aye. He flew by here a couple of minutes ago. Without so much as
             a by your leave.

VICTOR: Right. What ye
             daein'?

WINSTON: Oh, sorry. This is
             Chris, Thommo, Gillie,
             Pat and Tiffany.

             VICTOR SAYS HELLO
             TO THEM ALL. PAT
             AND TIFFANY ARE
             WINCHIN'.

WINSTON: As ye can see, Pat and Tiffany are an item.

VICTOR: What the hell are ye playin' at?

WINSTON: I'm barred from the Clansman. I've naewhere else tae go.

VICTOR: So ye're hangin' around wi' these mutants? Why don't ye just drink
             in the hoose?

WINSTON: Naw – it's company
             I'm missin'! I don't
             like drinkin' in the
             hoose on ma tod!
             Jackie Bird staring at
             ye as if ye're an alky
             . . . Huv ye tried
             this? (he offers Victor
             a bottle of brightly

             coloured gunk) Scadooba – Stawberry – 6% – Barbados trapped
             in a bottle.

VICTOR: What did Boabby bar ye fur?

WINSTON: Something over nuthin' really – I just said, 'Afternoon, Boabby.
             Pint of my usual, please.' He geid us it and it seemed a tad
             cloudy. I suggested maybe his pipes could do with a rinse out.
             He said it couldn't be that. I asked if I could be furnished with a
             fresh pint but Boabby for some reason asked me to leave.

DURING THIS DIALOGUE, WE CUT TO THE CLANSMAN AND SEE WINSTON ARGUING FURIOUSLY WITH BOABBY. HE TAKES A SIP OF HIS PINT AND SPITS IT OVER BOABBY. BOABBY COLLARS HIM AND BODILY REMOVES HIM FROM THE BAR.

VICTOR: Why don't ye just go tae Broon's?

WINSTON: Broons? The last time we were in there a guy got stabbed. Broon's is full of roasters.

VICTOR: That wis fifteen year ago, fur God's sake.

WINSTON: Nae chance. It's a toilet.

AT THAT POINT, THE KIDS HURL THEIR BOTTLES AGAINST THE WALL AND CHEER.

PAT: (addressing Winston) Ur ye comin' up tae Gillie's fur a gemme of *Gran Turismo* wi' us?

WINSTON: I suppose I could nick doon tae Broon's for a pint.

7. INT. JACK'S HOUSE. DAY.

JACK SITS ALONE AT HIS LITTLE KITCHEN TABLE. HE HAS A WEDDING PHOTOGRAPH OF HIMSELF AND JEAN IN HIS HANDS. VICTOR AND HIS WIFE ARE ALSO IN THE PHOTO WITH A COUPLE OF OTHER PEOPLE AS WELL. VICTOR SIDLES IN.

VICTOR: The door was open. What happened tae you back there?

JACK: I didnae gie a very guid impression, did I?

VICTOR: No. You gave an excellent impression. Of Jesse Owen! Right oot the shoppin' centre then on tae a bus!

JACK: Ach, ma bottle crashed. I'm past askin' anybody oot.

VICTOR: (noticing the photo on the table and picking it up) Christ, aye. That wis a rare day. Who's that big dame again?

JACK: That wis Janet Friel – the spinster, sure. Lived up the stairs fae us.

VICTOR: Oh, aye. Butter wouldnae melt, aye? Did she no' get pumped in the lavvy that day?

JACK: Aye. Winston's faither, sure – dirty auld bastart.

THEY LAUGH.

VICTOR: How long is Jean away noo?

JACK: Ten year in a fortnight.

VICTOR: Jesus. Ten year. That means ma Betty's deid twelve year.

JACK: Aye.

VICTOR: It's racin' away fae us noo, intit?

JACK: Aye. That's how I'm no' going through aw that again.

VICTOR: Jack. It's no' ma place tae tell ye how long a man should mourn – but ten years – ten years is plenty.

JACK: (pauses and then) Aye.

VICTOR: Goin' on a date doesnae mean ye're betrayin' Jean's memory. She'd want ye tae be happy. You get yersel' doon tae that shop and ask that woman out . . . And, besides . . . they diddies . . . oooooh.

THEY BOTH LAUGH.

8. EXT. BROON'S. DAY.

WINSTON STANDS LOOKING AT THE SIGN. IT READS 'THE POT STILL'. HE ENTERS.

9. INT. PUB. DAY.

WINSTON APPROACHES THE BAR, LOOKING AROUND, IMPRESSED. THERE IS A BARMAN IN PLACE, WEARING A WHITE APRON.

WINSTON: Here, did this no' use tae be Broon's?

BARMAN: That's right, sir. Changed hands years ago.

WINSTON: Oh, right.

WINSTON IS CONSIDERABLY CHEERED UP. THE PUB SEEMS LOVELY. A FIRE BURNS. AN OLDER COUPLE SIT CHATTING COMFORTABLY. A MIDDLE-AGED COUPLE ENJOY TASTY LOOKING PUB GRUB. A BARMAID PUTS DOWN A BRAND NEW ASHTRAY, A NEW BEER MAT AND A BOWL OF COMPLIMENTARY NUTS.

BARMAN: What'll it be, sir?

WINSTON: Eh. Pint of lager, please. Must be fifteen year since I wis in here last . . .

WINSTON LOOKS OVER TO SEE TWO YOUNG WELL-DRESSED MEN HAVING A QUIET GAME OF POOL.

BARMAN: Really? One pound thirty.

WINSTON: Oh. One-thirty. Smashin'. Nice clean pint, tae. This is a smashin' shop ye've got.

BARMAN: Thanks very much.

WINSTON LIFTS THE PINT TO HIS LIPS AND, IN THE GANTRY MIRROR, HE SPOTS THE PUB DOOR OPENING. A MASKED GUNMAN ENTERS, BRANDISHING A SAWN-OFF SHOTGUN. WINSTON TURNS BACK TO SEE THAT THE BARMAN  IS CROUCHED AND OUT OF SIGHT. HE TURNS BACK IN TIME TO SEE THE GUNMAN SHOOT ONE OF THE POOL PLAYERS CLEAN IN THE CHEST.

GUNMAN: That's a message fae Bobo Mitchell!!!!

THE GUNMAN RUNS OUT. WINSTON CALMLY PUTS HIS COAT ON.

WINSTON: See ye in another fifteen years.

10. EXT. SHOP. DAY.

JACK AND VICTOR ARE ABOUT TO ENTER THE SHOP.

JACK: De ye mind if I go in masel'?

VICTOR: Aye. On ye go. Wait a minute. (straightening Jack's tie) What are you gonnie say?

JACK: Hello, Barbara – Jack. It's lovely tae see ye again. Allow me to be straight with you. I've admired ye from afar for some time and it occurred to me, you and I are about the same age and, if you were free to do so, would you like to accompany me on a date? Perhaps a movie show or a meal or simply a drink. What do you say?

VICTOR: (impressed) Very good, Jack.

JACK TURNS ON HIS HEAD AND ENTERS THE SHOP. WE SEE HIS POV. IT IS A LONG WALK TO THE COUNTER. THE COUNTER SEEMS TO BE GETTING FURTHER AWAY. JACK'S FACE IS CONFIDENT, RESOLUTE. HE FINALLY ARRIVES AT THE COUNTER BUT HAS NOW LOST HIS IMPETOUS. BARBARA STANDS SMILING AT HIM.

JACK: Go out?

BARBARA: That would be lovely. When?

JACK: Thursday?

BARBARA: Ah. Thursday. I generally go out on Thursdays wi' ma sister.

JACK: Oh.

BARBARA: Wait! What about your pal? The four of us could go out.

JACK: Aye! Haud on a minute!

JACK SCUTTLES TO THE DOOR OF THE SHOP. HE POKES HIS HEAD OUT TO VICTOR.

VICTOR: How did ye get on?

JACK: How did we get on! She said aye! And she's got a sister!

11. INT. WINSTON'S FLAT. LATE NIGHT.

HE SITS IN HIS DRESSING GOWN HAVING JUST FINISHED A
MASSIVE BOOK. HE SIGHS AND SWITCHES ON THE TV WITH
THE REMOTE AND *CHEERS* COMES ON. THE THEME TUNE IS
JUST ENDING. HE OPENS A CAN OF BEER.

VOICE OVER:
Noooorm!

NORM: (voice over) Aliens have taken over my stomach and they're
demanding beer. (laugh) Ye know I love this bar. My friends, if, for
some reason, I couldn't come here every day, why I think I would
probably kill myself.

OTHER CUSTOMER:
(voice over) I'd kill myself too. Not being able to come to your regular
bar? Life wouldn't be worth living!

WINSTON TURNS OFF THE TELLY.

WINSTON: Right.

12. EXT. BUS STOP. EVENING.

JACK AND VICTOR
STAND WAITING.
JACK LOOKS AT HIS
WATCH.

JACK: They're no' comin'.
They've gave us a
dissie.

VICTOR: Relax. They'll be here.
It's the bus that's late.

JACK: Aye. It'll be that speccy bastard. Drives the bus at two miles an hoor
cause he's blind.

A DOUBLE DECKER BUS INCHES OVER THE HILL AT TWO
MILES AN HOUR.

VICTOR: Op. Here we go. You were right enough.

AS THE BUS PULLS UP, WE SEE THE DRIVER HAS COKE-
BOTTLE GLASSES. HE PEERS OUT THE WINDSHIELD, HIS EYES
ALL SQUINTY.
EIGHT PEOPLE GET OFF THE BUS.

JACK: Ye nervous?

VICTOR: Aye. I've every right tae be nervous. I huvnae a clue what this sister
            looks like.

            A TEENAGE COUPLE GET OFF. A LONE TEENAGER GETS OFF.
            A MAN WITH A PAPER GETS OFF. WE KEEP CUTTING BACK TO
            JACK AND VICTOR. THEIR EXPECTATION IS MOUNTING. THEN
            A REALLY OLD PENSIONER TAKES FOREVER GETTING OFF.
            CUT TO JACK AND VICTOR, WILLING THIS WOMAN OFF THE
            BUS.

JACK: This is like Chinese water torture!

            DIRECTLY BEHIND THE PENSIONER IS BARBARA AND A VERY
            PRESENTABLE OLDER LADY. VICTOR SWELLS UP.

VICTOR: Oh, helllooooo.

            BARBARA STEPS UP.

BARBARA: Hello, Jack. Hello,
            Victor. This is my
            sister, Edith.

            VICTOR GOES TO
            SHAKE THE NICE-
            LOOKING WOMAN'S
            HAND. SHE WALKS
            PAST HIM AND
            THERE STANDS A
            FOUR-AND-A-HALF-
            FOOT UGLY WEE
            BASTARD. VICTOR IS
            CRUSHED BEYOND
            REPAIR. HE FIXES A
            SMILE TO HIDE HIS
            DISGUST.

13. INT. CLANSMAN. NIGHT.

TAM IS BUYING TWO PINTS. BOABBY EYES HIM SUSPICIOUSLY AS HE GIVES HIM THEM.

BOABBY: Who's the other one fur?

TAM: (lying) Me. I've got a right drouth. Mad wi' the thirst. It's a sandal. An Arab's sandal. Dry. Bone dry.

HE EXHALES AS IF TO DEMONSTRATE AS HE BACKS OFF WITH THE PINTS.

14. EXT. CLANSMAN. NIGHT.

WINSTON IS STANDING OUTSIDE TRYING TO GET A HEAT. TAM POKES HIS HEAD OUT.

TAM: Here. Hurry up. Take this. Ye'll get me bloody barred an' all.

WINSTON: Cheers. That's smashin'.

TAM: Why don't ye just come in and make yer apologies?

WINSTON: He can whistle fur it. I'm no' apologising. This'll dae me fine. When ye go back in tell big Arthur tae sit on his arse so I can see the fitba an aw.

TAM DISAPPEARS BACK INSIDE. JACK AND VICTOR APPEAR WITH THEIR DATES. JACK HOLDS THE DOOR OPEN FOR THE LADIES.

WINSTON: Hello, lads.

WINSTON IS CRANING TO GET A LOOK AT VICTOR'S DATE. VICTOR IS TRYING TO OBSCURE HER WITH HIS COAT BUT WINSTON STICKS HIS PAW IN.

WINSTON: Hello, ladies. I'm Winston.

WINSTON STARES INCREDULOUSLY AT EDITH.

BOTH: Hello, Winston.

THE LADIES DISAPPEAR INSIDE THE PUB.

JACK: Are you still barred?

WINSTON: Aye. Which one of you unlucky bastards is saddled wi' the munchkin?

VICTOR: Right. That's it.

VICTOR GOES TO ENTER BUT DOES AN ABOUT-TURN. JACK GRABS HIM.

JACK: Where are you gaun?

VICTOR: Hame. I'm no' sittin' in ma local wi' that thing. I'll never hear the end of it!

JACK: You're gaun AWOL and leavin' me wi' these two women?

VICTOR: I only saw one woman. I dunno what the other one wis.

WINSTON: A munchkin, sure.

JACK: Shut up. Gie it a chance. Bail me oot here.

VICTOR: Right. But you owe me.

JACK: Aye, aye, aye. (to Winston) Are ye wantin' anything brought oot?

WINSTON: Bag of nuts.

JACK: Big bag or a wee bag?

WINSTON: Wee bag. Just like Victor's!

VICTOR DRAWS HIM A STINKER. THEY ENTER THE CLANSMAN.

15. INT. CLANSMAN. NIGHT.

JACK AND VICTOR SIDLE UP TO THE BAR. THE WOMEN STAND BEHIND THEM.

BOABBY IS PUTTING UP WHISKY BOTTLES INTO THE OPTICS.
HE TURNS ROUND STILL WITH ONE BOTTLE IN HAND.

BOABBY: Jack. Victor. What are youse two daein' in at this time?

JACK: We're out with a couple of friends if it was any of yer business. When are ye lettin' Winston back in?

BOABBY: When he apologises. Aren't you going to introduce me?

BOTH: Certainly. Naw!

JACK: (stepping aside to reveal the two women) Boabby, this is Barbara and Edith.

BOABBY: Hello, Barbara. Hello . . .

UPON SEEING EDITH,
BOABBY TAKES A
FRIGHT AND DROPS
THE BOTTLE OF
WHISKY.

BOABBY: (off guard) Right. Right. What are yis fur?

JACK: Usual for us and eh . . .

BARBARA: Gin and tonic.

EDITH: Pint of Guinness.

BOABBY: Take a seat. I'll bring it ower.

THEY GO TO SIT DOWN. THEY HAVE TO PASS ARTHUR WHO
GETS UP WHEN THEY PASS. HE IS A GIANT. THE WOMEN
FACE AWAY FROM THE BAR WHILE JACK AND VICTOR SIT
AGAINST THE WALL.

JACK: Hello, Arthur.

ARTHUR: Jack. Victor.

VICTOR: What's the score?

ARTHUR: 2–1 Chelsea.

             WE HEAR A BANGING AT THE WINDOW. ARTHUR TURNS
             ROUND TO SEE WINSTON MOTIONING HIM TO SIT ON HIS
             ARSE. ARTHUR FLICKS HIM THE VICK. BOABBY SEES THIS AND
             GOES OVER TO THE WINDOW WITH A POSTER.

BOABBY: (speaking through the glass to Winston) Are you apologising?

             WINSTON MOTIONS HIM TO THE WINDOW WITH APOLOGETIC
             FACE. BOABBY LEANS IN. WINSTON SPLASHES HIS PINT AT
             THE WINDOW.

WINSTON: 'Ere's yer apology, ya prick.

BOABBY: Ye're still barred.

             BOABBY PUTS A POSTER UP AND OBSCURES HIS VISION. A
             GOAL IS SCORED. THE PUB CHEERS.

ARTHUR: 2–2! Ya beauty!

BARBARA: Is this yer local, aye?

JACK: (distracted by the
             football) Eh. Aye.
             We've been comin'
             here for long and
             weary.

BOABBY: (whispering) Victor . . .

             DURING THIS, BOABBY IS MIMING THE SHAGGING GESTURE
             WITH HIS HANDS TO ANNOY VICTOR.

VICTOR: So, Edith, um, de ye work in the shop along wi' Barbara?

EDITH: Naw.

VICTOR: Right. So . . .

EDITH: Sew . . .

VICTOR: So . . .

EDITH: Sew. I dae alterations an' 'at. Sewin'.

BOABBY ARRIVES WITH THE DRINKS.

BOABBY: There ye go, ladies and gentlemen . . . £6.80.

JACK: Here, Edith, you might want tae alter his price list!

THEY ALL LAUGH APART FROM VICTOR.

JACK: Did ye catch that one, Victor? I'm sayin' what wi' Edith daein'
            alterations, she might want tae alter the prices in here.

VICTOR: Aye. Good yin.

WE CUT TO
VICTOR'S POV. HE
SEES EDITH SITTING
DIRECTLY IN FRONT
OF HIM. BEHIND HER,
ARE THREE
REGULARS AIR
HUMPING AND
DOING QUASIMODO
IMPRESSIONS. JACK
SEES THIS. BARBARA
SEES JACK SEEING IT AND TURNS ROUND WONDERING WHAT
IS GOING ON. THE THREE IMMEDIATELY DISPERSE IN THE
NICK OF TIME.

16. EXT. BUS STOP. NIGHT.

BARBARA: That wis lovely, Jack.

JACK: I fair enjoyed masel'. Ye're guid company. Aren't they guid company,
            Victor?

VICTOR: Guid company.

BARBARA: Here's oor bus. I'll see you soon, Jack.

BARBARA LEANS
FORWARD TO KISS
JACK ON THE
CHEEK. JACK
CHUCKLES AWAY
EMBARASSED. EDITH
GOES TO DO THE
SAME TO VICTOR,
WHO SHAKES HER
HAND WITH ONE
HAND AND RUBS
HER HEAD WITH THE
OTHER.

VICTOR: There ye are then.
            G'night.

THEY BOARD THE
BUS AND SIT DOWN.
BARBARA MAKES
THE PHONE MIME OUT THE WINDOW AT JACK. VICTOR BENDS
OVER, EYES SHUT TIGHT.

JACK: 'Smatter, Victor? Ye alright?

VICTOR: I'm fine. I'm just trying tae get that ugly bastard's image oot ma heid.

JACK: (pointing at Victor) Now you listen here . . . (sounding defeated) Aye.
            There's no gettin' away from it. She wis a gargoyle. Hard tae believe
            that, intit? One could be so lovely and the other one would gie ye
            the boak.

VICTOR: Imagine doing the dirty wi' that.

JACK: Don't – I'll no' sleep the night.

VICTOR: What's yer next move then?

JACK: Well, if she phones, I'll take it from there. And will you be seeing . . .

VICTOR: NO!

JACK: Didnae think so.

17. INT. JACK'S HOUSE. DAY

JACK IS IN A CHIPPER MOOD. HE'S SINGING 'BEAUTIFUL DOLL' AS HE POLISHES HIS SHOES.

JACK: Oooh, you beautiful doll . . .

THE DOORBELL GOES. JACK GOES TO IT. HE LOOKS THROUGH THE PEEPHOLE. VICTOR STANDS THERE, PRESENTING A LOAF.

JACK: Oh, Victor.

JACK OPENS THE DOOR.

JACK: Hi, Victor.

VICTOR: 'Mon, Jack. Thursday morning – let's hit the park and fatten up they ducks.

JACK: I cannae.

VICTOR: What de ye mean ye cannae? It's Thursday. Park day.

JACK: I'm actually going to the park wi' Barbara.

VICTOR: Oh, right.

JACK: So, eh . . .

JACK EYES THE LOAF. VICTOR, RESIGNED, HANDS IT OVER.

JACK: I'll see ye efter.

VICTOR: Aye. Enjoy yersel'.

WHAT FOLLOWS IS A MONTAGE SEQUENCE.
VICTOR SITS AT THE BAR. HE LOOKS OVER TO THE QUIZ MACHINE WHERE JACK AND BARBARA ARE HAVING A RIGHT

GOOD LAUGH. CUT TO JACK AND BARBARA HAVING A
LOVELY SPAGHETTI LUNCH IN A NICE CAFÉ. CUT TO VICTOR
HAVING AN EGG ROLL AND TEA IN A SHITEY ONE. THE EGG
SQUIRTS INTO HIS TEA. CUT TO JACK'S DOORSTEP. VICTOR
RINGS HIS BELL. JACK ANSWERS. VICTOR EXCITEDLY HOLDS
UP THE RACING POST, POINTING TO A NAG. JACK, IN THE
MIDDLE OF SHAVING, GENTLY REBUFFS HIM AND CLOSES
THE DOOR. CUT TO VICTOR MAKING TWO BREWS. HE
REALISES HE ONLY NEEDS ONE AND POURS THE OTHER
DOWN THE SINK. CUT TO A COMMUNITY HALL. WE SEE JACK
AND BARBARA PLAYING TABLE TENNIS. THEY ARE HAVING A
WONDERFUL TIME. WE PAN OVER TO ANOTHER TABLE TO
SEE VICTOR SERVING TO AN ANCIENT OLD MAN WHO
SWINGS ONE SECOND TOO LATE TO HIT THE BALL. HE IS
CLEARLY AN UNFIT OPPONENT. VICTOR TODDLES OFF TO
RETRIEVE IT.

18. INT. NAVID'S SHOP. DAY.

NAVID IS SERVING
VICTOR.

NAVID: Brillo pads, eggs . . .
           toilet roll. Just one big
           KitKat?

VICTOR: Aye. What of it?

NAVID: You normally get two big KitKats – one for you, one for Jack.

VICTOR: We dinnae dae everythin' together. We urnae joined at the hip, ye
           know.

NAVID: Oh. Fell oot. Bad news. You cannae afford tae be fallin' oot wi' yer
           pals at your age.

VICTOR: Why would that be, Trisha?

NAVID: You are an old man. You could die in the night and then you and
           Jack would be in separate worlds with unfinished business.
           (extending a hand) Two-twenty.

ISA GHOSTS IN. BOTH NAVID AND VICTOR JUMP.

ISA: Hello, Victor.

VICTOR: (under his breath) Jesus. Hello, Isa.

ISA: Where's yer wee pal the day?

NAVID: I think they've fell oot.

VICTOR: We huvnae fallen oot.

ISA: Lucky Donkey, Navid.

VICTOR: Oh, aye. I'll take a Lucky Donkey an' aw.

NAVID: Two Donkeys.

ISA: Ye'll be at a bit o' a loose end wi' Jack trippin' the light fantastic wi' that Barbara sort.

THEY BOTH SCRATCH THEIR SCRATCH CARDS. NEITHER WINS ANYTHING.

VICTOR: Naw – good luck to them.

ISA: Victor. I've got something tae tell ye.

VICTOR: What, Isa?

ISA TURNS VICTOR AWAY FROM NAVID.

ISA: This Barbara – she's . . .

VICTOR: Don't tell me. She's the Black Widow.

ISA: No, no. She's . . . eh . . .

NAVID: A junkie?

VICTOR: A lap dancer who fires ping-pong balls ootae her duff fur cash, at a club in the toon.

NAVID GOES INTO HYSTERICS.

NAVID: That's a cracker.
Right oot the duff.
(miming the act)
Pung. Pung. Pung.

ISA: You know how I don't
like gossip?

NAVID: Aye, ye dae.

ISA: I wis at the doctor's this morning – women's troubles – and who else
is sittin' but Elsie Clark. She's got angina, right enough. Wee soul.
Her livin' alone an' all. Her daughter works in Tesco's and her manager
is Alec Wilson. Remember him? Fella that drinks too much? Everyone
thought he wis gay, turned oot he wisnae? Well he started a
Saturday boy. Nice boy. Bad wi' the acne. He'd been in the Terries
and hud goat pally wi' Norma Flynn's boy Rab wi' the funny hon like
a claw. Aw the weans used tae call him Rab the Crab, de ye mind?
Well his girlfriend's mother was throwing oot an auld tea set that her
granny hud left her. It wis perfectly good but she didnae need it so
she she gied it tae Rab tae take into the charity shop up at the
precinct. But Rab says, 'Haud on, I don't need tae go up the toon.
I wash that wummin's man's car – I'll take it up her hoose.' So he
did. But she wasnae in. So her man took in the tea set.

VICTOR: Who's man took in the
tea set?

ISA: Barbara's man. She's
married.

19. INT. BINGO HALL. DAY.

JACK AND BARBARA WANDER INTO THE BODY OF THE HALL.
JACK IS LOOKING FOR A COUPLE OF SEATS FOR HIMSELF
AND BARBARA.

BARBARA: How many books did ye get?

JACK: Two.

BARBARA: One each? That's not very much.

JACK: That's plenty. Any mair than that and ye end up busier than a one arm cabbie wi' crabs.

BARBARA: (chuckling) Jack . . .
Right, I'll away and get the coffees.

JACK SPOTS WINSTON WHO IS SITTING DOWN WITH FOUR WOMEN. HE HAS EIGHT BOOKS. THEY ARE LAID OUT. HE IS NONCHALANTLY SIPPING A PINT, EATING A BURGER AND A PLATE OF CHIPS WHILST STAMPING OFF HIS NUMBERS LIKE A PROFESSIONAL.

JACK: Op. Winston. What are you daein' in here?

WINSTON: Naewhere else tae go.

JACK: Oh, aye. (watching Winston's expertise) Hey, ye're guid at that.

WINSTON: That's what a week oot the Clansman does fur ye.

JACK: Has it been a week already?

WINSTON: Longest week of ma life. I'm about demented trying tae occupy masel'. This mornin' I had the crossword done, taught masel' chess and papered the fireplace wall before I hud ma first shite of the day.

JACK: Ye missed yersel' in there on Thursday. Ye know how Big Stevie's aye bettin'. Well he bet Alfie he could juggle three tumblers. So Alfie, who's half-cut, stomps behind the bar gets three tumblers and says if ye can dae it, I'll buy the whole pub a drink. But what Alfie doesnae realise is that Stevie is full of that red stuff. Aftershock. He'd been in there since five bells. So up he gets on tap of the stool, tumblers in hand . . .

JACK REALISES WINSTON IS EVILLING HIM.

JACK: It wis shite. Ye never missed yersel' at all.

WOMAN 1:   Here. Did ye see Larry Hagman on Lorraine Kelly this mornin'?

WINSTON: Naw.

WOMAN 2:   I saw it. He's lookin' his age, int he?

WINSTON: Is he? I thought he aye looked efter issel'.

JACK: You need tae get yersel' back in the Clansman.

WINSTON: Mmn. I see ye're in wi' big Boobra.

JACK: Barbara.

WINSTON: Whatever. Are ye seein' much o' Victor?

JACK: Aye. Naw.

WINSTON: Oh, aye. Gein' 'im a wide berth since ye hooked up wi' yer fancy piece? That's poor.

JACK: What's poor?

WINSTON: Leavin' Victor hung oot tae dry like that. Don't get me wrang – if I wis gettin' some hole flung at me, I'd be distracted an' aw but ye've got tae remember yer pals.

JACK: It's no' like that wi' me an' Barbara. We're just companions.

          A WOMAN SLINKS BY. SHE OPENS A BAG.

WOMAN: Yis wantin' any Armani specs? I've goat Hugo Boss an' aw there.

ALL: No' the day, hen. Ye're alright.

SHE SLINKS OFF.
BARBARA RETURNS
WITH TWO COFFEES.

BARBARA: Queue wis murder.
          Hello, there.
          Winston, isn't it?

WINSTON: Hello, hen.

THE WOMAN SITTING NEXT TO WINSTON SHOUTS UP.

WOMAN: House!!! (to Winston) I'm normally aye waitin' on wan an' aw!!!

WINSTON: No' the day though, eh? Guid fur you. (under his breath) Jammy cow.
          Right. I'm away. Goodbye, ladies. Right, Jack. I'll see ye. I've a
          clarinet lesson at two.

WINSTON EXITS
SHOT. HE RE-
ENTERS AND LEANS
IN.

WINSTON: It's aw about where
          ye put yer fingers, ye
          know?

WINSTON EXITS.

20. INT. CHARITY SHOP. DAY.

BARBARA IS SORTING STUFF. VICTOR ENTERS.

BARBARA: Hello, Victor.

VICTOR: Hello, Barbara.

BARBARA: Cloudy the day, intit?

VICTOR: Aye. Cloudy. I want
          ma pal back.

BARBARA: What do you mean?

VICTOR: You know fine what I mean. You've no' right bein' wi' him. Ye're
          married.

BARBARA: Oh. Right. That.

VICTOR: What de ye think ye're
          playin' at? Jack's ten
          years' widowed. Ye
          cannae be tinkerin' wi
          somone's feelin's like
          that.

BARBARA: Listen, Victor. The last thing I was gonnie dae was hurt Jack. He's great company and that's all there is to it.

VICTOR: What's yer hubby got tae say aboot that? AAAH. He doesnae know!

JACK: Doesnae know what?

           VICTOR AND BARBARA START AT JACK'S VOICE.

VICTOR: Doesnae know what tae . . . charge fur ma . . . cardigan . . . z.

JACK: What are you daein' in here?

VICTOR: Bringin' in mair claes – cardigans.

           VICTOR HOLDS UP A WOMAN'S PINK CARDY.

JACK: Oh, right. Barbara . . . Now. Tonight. How does this sound? Pepper steak?

BARBARA: Um. Tonight?

JACK: Aye. How? De ye huv plans?

BARBARA: No. Tonight's fine.

JACK: Victor? Tonight alright for you too?

VICTOR: Eh?

JACK: Aye. I thought the three of us could sit doon.

VICTOR: Naw. Naw. Dae yer own thing. I'm no' wantin' tae . . . youse'll huv . . . eh . . . three's a crowd, Jack.

JACK: I wis always gonnie ask ye.

VICTOR: So ye were. What's fur puddin'? Gooseberries?

           JACK HAS PRODUCED THE STEAKS FROM THE BAG.

JACK: Exhibit A. Read 'em and weep. Three steaks. What do you say?

VICTOR: Eh. Aye.

BARBARA: Aye.

21. INT. JACK'S FLAT. NIGHT.

>   VICTOR SITS IN SILENCE IN THE LIVING ROOM. JACK
>   EMERGES WITH A CUP OF TEA.

VICTOR: (sipping) Is there sugar in this?

JACK: Sorry. Barbara takes a sugar.

>   JACK GOES BACK INTO THE KITCHEN.

JACK: Saw Winston earlier on.

VICTOR: Aye.

JACK: Still barred fae the Clansman.

VICTOR: Really.

JACK: Ye're affa quiet.

VICTOR: Nae reason.

JACK: Are ye in the huff 'cause of me and Barbara?

VICTOR: No. That's no' it, Jack.

JACK: Well what's the matter wi' ye?

VICTOR: Sit doon. I've
             something tae tell ye.
             I'm yer pal and ye
             need tae know.

             THE PHONE RINGS.

JACK: 2470. Barbara. Hello.
             Where are ye? . . .

JACK, IN SILENCE, LEARNS ABOUT BARBARA WHO TELLS ALL. DURING THIS CONVERSATION VICTOR GOES INTO THE KITCHEN TO SPARE JACK'S EMBARRASSMENT AND TO WATCH THE GAS. JACK REPLACES HAND SET. VICTOR EMERGES TO SEE JACK SITTING GLUM AT THE TABLE. HE PUTS DOWN TWO PLATES. THE CENTRE PLATE HAS THREE STEAKS WITH PEPPER SAUCE ON. AS THEY SPEAK, VICTOR DISHES UP A STEAK EACH.

JACK: That wis Barbara.

VICTOR: Aye.

JACK: She'll no' be coming.

VICTOR: Naw.

JACK: She's eh . . .

VICTOR: I know. Sorry, Jack.

AS VICTOR SPEAKS HE CUTS THE REMAINING STEAK IN HALF AND PLACES A BIT ON EACH OF THE TWO PLATES.

JACK: That's alright, Victor.

22. INT. CLANSMAN. NIGHT.

JACK AND VICTOR ENTER.

BOABBY: Oh, look – there's Richard and Judy in . . .

BOTH: Shut up, baw bag.

THEY SIT AT THE BAR.

VICTOR: That was a rare meal Jackie boy. I'm stuffed.

JACK: Aye. Me tae. Full as a welk.

WINSTON: Nice tae see youse
            two pally again.

            JACK AND VICTOR
            LOOK ROUND. THEY
            DOUBLE TAKE THE
            MAN IN LONG COAT,
            BUNNET, THICK
            GLASSES AND A
            ROPEY MOUSTACHE.
            IT'S WINSTON.

JACK: Winston?!

WINSTON: Keep cool. Ye'll blow
            ma cover.

VICTOR: Two pints, Boabby.

WINSTON: Three.

VICTOR: Three . . . pints.

JACK: What ye playin' at?

WINSTON: He's no' winnin'. I'll sit here, nice as ye like – the perfect customer.
            And he'll be nane the wiser.

VICTOR: And naebody's tippled?

WINSTON: Youse two didnae.

            VICTOR AND JACK'S PINTS ARE PLONKED IN FRONT OF THEM.
            WINSTON'S PINT IS OBVIOUSLY CLOUDY SLOPS. WINSTON
            LOSES THE PLOT AND WHIPS OFF HIS GLASSES. HIS
            MOUSTACHE COMES
            AWAY.

WINSTON: Right, you, ya
            bastart. That's
            exactly whit I'm on
            aboot. That pint's a
            disgrace, ya robbin'
            bastard!

BOABBY: I knew that would bring ye out! I knew that wis you!!!

THE WHOLE PUB LAUGHS.

CLOSING MUSIC AND CREDITS, THEN:

WINSTON LIES IN HIS BED. HE WAKES, BADLY HUNGOVER BUT SELF-SATISFIED.

WINSTON: (Thought voice over as he checks his pulse.) It's guid tae be livin'. Oh, I've missed that place. Oh, ma heid. What a night. I'll just take another wee hof oor.

HE TURNS OVER AND IS FACE TO FACE WITH EDITH THE UGLY SISTER.

CUT TO BLACK.

4. WADDIN'.

This episode showcases one of *Still Game*'s most popular characters, Navid. Everybody loves a wedding and we're no exception. The year before this episode was written, we attended the wedding of the actor who plays Navid, Sanjeev Kohli. It was an absolute belter and it led directly to the conception of this episode. All of Craiglang are desperate to be invited to the Asian society wedding of the year and Navid knows that his hallowed invites are worth their weight in gold. This main storyline is coupled with the introduction of the character of Wullie Macintosh, the tight-fisted tapper who returns from the dead.

We enjoy a special effect. So you'll notice that, any time one of the rare invites is opened, the opener is bathed in a beautiful gold light, while sitar music gently strums

in the background. We loved this idea and the gold light is a direct steal from one of our favourite films, *Pulp Fiction*, where John Travolta can be seen opening a briefcase, the contents of which are never disclosed. He is bathed in a gold light when he looks in it and we thought, 'Nice touch. We'll have that.'

As far as audience appreciation goes, Navid gets a ton of it. So, it is at this point in the book that we would like to issue all you readers and other cast members a stark reminder. With yer Navids, yer Winstons, yer Tams, yer Boabbys and yer Isas, these characters are finely honed and crafted – BY US. And, just as we give, we can also just as abruptly take away. Understood? Good.

Ford and Greg

WADDIN'.

1. INT. JACK'S HOUSE. DAY.

JACK AND VICTOR ARE WATCHING TELEVISION.

JACK: Victor! C'mere tae ye see this! Quick! It's nearly away!

VICTOR: What? What?

JACK: Look at that toaster. De Longhi. Four-slice. Crumb drawer. Cool touch walls – the Rolls Royce of toasters. I'm gonnie get wan o' them.

VICTOR: Anything would be better than that heap of shit ye've had fur the last forty year.

JACK: That's served me well. That's a Thorn. It's got four settin's!

VICTOR: Aye. Black, black, black and burnt. Turn over.

2. EXT. LANDING. DAY.

WINSTON EXITS THE LIFT. HE BUMPS INTO ISA.

WINSTON: Isa. Where are you off tae?

ISA: Navid's. Tae dae ma shift.

WINSTON: Right. See ye.

THE LIFT DOORS BEGIN TO CLOSE. WINSTON HEADS FOR JACK'S DOOR.

WINSTON: That wis close. I got aff lightly there.

THE LIFT DINGS, THE DOOR OPENS AGAIN. ISA POPS OUT.

ISA: I'm glad I caught ye. I completely forgot to tell you.

WINSTON: Tell me what, Isa?

ISA: Well I never buy *The Times*. There's usually nothin' in it that ye huvnae read in the real papers. Just the same auld news again, later on. Rubbish really. So there's nae point in payin' twice fur it. Anyway, I don't know why but I bought one.

DURING THIS SPEIL, WINSTON IS MIMING USING A REMOTE CONTROL.

ISA: And I'm lookin' through it and somethin' leaps oot at me. What are ye daein?

WINSTON: I'm tryin' tae fast forward you tae the punchline.

ISA: What?

WINSTON: What is the end of this story?

ISA: Well, I wis looking . . .

WINSTON: The end!

ISA: At the intimations section . . .

WINSTON: The end, mind!

ISA: Wullie Macintosh is deid.

WINSTON: Oh.

3. INT. JACK'S HOUSE. DAY.

DOORBELL RINGS.

JACK: Aye, come on in. The door's open.

WINSTON PLONKS HIMSELF DOWN, PICKING UP A BISCUIT.

WINSTON: Look at this – Fox's Classics. Ye aye get a right snobby poofy biscuit at Jack's, don't ye, Victor?

VICTOR: I brung them.

WINSTON: Did ye? Tasty, but. I love the . . . um . . . the way, the chocolatey . . .

VICTOR: That's plenty.

WINSTON: Wullie Macintosh is deid.

JACK: Eh?

WINSTON: Aye. Isa saw it in the paper. Died in the hospital.

JACK: When are they plantin' him?

WINSTON: It's the cremmy. Thursday.

VICTOR: That bastard was intae me fur thirty quid.

WINSTON: Get in line. I fitted his cooker and he never squared me up fur it.

JACK: I'm sure I lent him somethin'. What was it noo? I cannae mind. I did lend him somethin', but.

WINSTON TEARS THE FOIL OFF A FRESH BISCUIT.

4. INT. NAVID'S SHOP. DAY.

NAVID IS FINISHING UP A PHONE CALL.

NAVID: Magic. Magic. Magic. That's quality. Thank you.

NAVID HANGS UP.

NAVID: Meena, that's the cars sorted. Mercedes-Benz – S-Class. Fantastic, eh?

MEENA IS AT THE END OF THE SHOP SITTING ON AN UPTURNED MILK CRATE, READING THE *INDIA TIMES.* SHE GRUNTS IN ACKNOWLEDGMENT.

NAVID: (mumbling) Don't get too excited. Arsehole.

HAVING HEARD THIS, MEENA LAUNCHES A VERBAL TIRADE AT NAVID IN THEIR NATIVE LANGUAGE.

NAVID: Stop it, Meena – I'm shitin' masel'. Look at me. I'm quaking in ma boots. Come ahead then, Meena. Come ahead, then. Ye can give me a kickin' when ye can move yer fat arse aff that crate!!

ISA: That's Wullie Macintosh deid.

NAVID: Who?

ISA: Wullie Macintosh. Wi' the Gorbachev mark on his heid.

NAVID: Eh?

ISA: (leaning in to be discreet) Like a bird shat blood oan his heid.

NAVID: Ooh. Wullie Macintosh.

NAVID DOES A SPLAT NOISE ON HIS HEAD BY WAY OF RECOGNITION.

NAVID: Oh, fur god sake. Meena . . .

MEENA: (from behind her newspaper) Uh?

NAVID: (in his own dialect) That's Wullie Macintosh deid.

MEENA: Who?

NAVID DOES THE SPLAT MIME. MEENA GRUNTS IN RECOGNITION.

NAVID: He's oan ma tick list.

ISA: Tick list fur what?

NAVID: He owed me eleven quid. Ach well. That's the gypsy creams up two
            pence a packet.

ISA: (mop in hand) That's me done.

NAVID: Right-o, Isa.

ISA: Heard ye oan the phone there.Ye've got the cars then fur . . .

NAVID: (mildly amused) Yes, Isa. The weddin'.

ISA: Mercedes-Benz.

NAVID: S-Class.

ISA: Oh, luxury. So what
            days de ye want me
            next week? Monday,
            Wednesday, Friday?

NAVID: No, Isa. No' Friday.

ISA: Oh, yes, that's right.
            The weddin'.

NAVID: Right, Isa. Let's you and I dispense with the verbal sparring. Next
            Friday is the wedding of the year in our community. Everyone
            who's anybody will be there. The Jaffir family's going. The Singhs
            are going, the Kumars and even the Ashoka people are coming
            and a few valued customers from this shop will be invited. Now
            you, Isa, are a nosy bastard.

ISA: Now wait . . .

NAVID: Fact, not insult. It's only natural that you should peddle about angling
            in desperation to be one of the lucky few.

HE PRESENTS TWO
ENVELOPES

NAVID: Now, in one of these envelopes is your wages from last week – in the other, an invite to the Asian society wedding of the year. Pick one and forfeit the other.

ISA SWEATS OVER HER CHOICE. SHE REACHES FOR ONE, HESITATES, REACHES FOR THE OTHER. NAVID PULLS THEM BOTH BACK, CHUCKLING.

NAVID: Look at the state ye're in. Aw jangling. I'm just pulling yer pisser, Isa. They are both for you.

ISA TAKES BOTH ENVELOPES. SHE OPENS THE FIRST ONE. IT'S HER WAGES. SHE OPENS THE SECOND. IT'S THE INVITE. ITS GILT EDGE CASTS A GOLD LIGHT ON ISA'S FACE WHICH IS ECSTATIC. WE HEAR A FAINT STRUM OF SITAR MUSIC.

5. EXT. SPARE GROUND. DAY.

JACK AND VICTOR SAUNTER ACROSS THE WASTELAND.

JACK: Four slices aw toastin' at the one time. Simultaneously. In tandem wi' each other.

VICTOR: Jack. Fur God's sake. Gie the toaster a break.

JACK: Wullie Macintosh, eh?

VICTOR: Aye. He was in my class at school. Snottery wee bastard he was. Aye havin' nosebleeds.

JACK: Nae family. I wish I could remember what it was I lent him.

VICTOR: Winston has a key to his house, does he not?

JACK: Aye, that's right. He was feedin' the cat when Wullie was in the hospital.

VICTOR: So we could get in – if we wanted.

JACK: Here, now. Ye're no' suggestin' we rummage through a deid man's hoose.

VICTOR: Yep.

JACK: That's a crackin' idea. What wi' him havin' nae family, it's nigh on the perfect rummaging scenario.

VICTOR: If there's any money lyin' aboot I'm due the first thirty quid.

JACK: That's a given.

ISA APPEARS IN THE SHOT. JACK AND VICTOR START.

ISA: Hello, lads. Wullie Macintosh is deid.

JACK: Fur once in your life, Isa, yer news is second hand.

VICTOR: Winston telt us.

ISA: Terrible, eh?

BOTH: Aye. Oh, aye.

ISA: It's terrible tae say but there he's deid and he never geid me back a guid calor gas heater I lent him.

JACK: Oh, dear, that wisnae like him.

ISA: Ideally, if there wis a key, I could go up there and get it back . . .

VICTOR: Aye, ye could. Right enough.

JACK: If ye had such a thing as a key . . .

VICTOR: A key would be handy.

            WINSTON ARRIVES.

ISA: Hello, Winston. I wis just sayin Wullie hud ma heater. A key would be handy.

WINSTON: I've got a key.

            JACK AND VICTOR DIG HIM IN THE RIBS.

WINSTON: For ma hoose – which is handy, fur gettin' oot and in. Otherwise I'd huv tae use the windae – which would be pish.

ISA: That's smashin' fur ye. I'll away. Ooh. Before I forget – look at this.

            SHE PRODUCES THE INVITE. AGAIN WE HEAR THE SITAR.

VICTOR: Jesus. It's beautiful.

JACK: What is it?

WINSTON: That, boys, is an invite to Navid's daughter's weddin'.

VICTOR: I heard aboot that. Ya jammy bastart. How did ye get yer hands on that?

ISA: (as she's leaving) He's invitin' a few select friends and customers.

JACK: Is he? Well, I better be gettin' one. I'm never out of his shop.

VICTOR: Me an' aw. I'm a select friend and customer. Hof ma pension goes right intae his till!

ISA: See yis efter!

JACK: (turning to Winston) Lucky old boot. Have you been asked?

WINSTON: No' yet. But I'll be there. I'll definitely be there.

VICTOR: How'z 'at?

WINSTON: Never you mind. But let's just say Wullie Mac's givin' me a gift fae the grave and I'll be gaun up tae get it.

              HE DANGLES THE KEY.

JACK: Aye, well, we'll be coming wi' ye. He's got stuff belangin' tae everyone. We'll need tae start a list.

6. EXT. STREET. DAY.

JACK AND VICTOR ARE CROSSING THE ROAD. A VAN SPEEDS TOWARDS THEM.

VICTOR: What's Winston on aboot? Aw that 'gift fae the grave' pish.

JACK: Dunno. Maybe Wullie hud a shotgun belongin' tae him and he's gonnie shoot his way intae the weddin'.

VICTOR: It'd kill me if that bastart gets gaun and we dinnae.

VICTOR: Haw.

JACK: Jesus! Are you blind, ya bastard?

TAM: You, ya old duffer! Get aff the road ya dosy pri . . . Jack! Victor! How about yis, ye're looking weel!

VICTOR: Tam, fur Christ's sake. What are you daein' drivin' a van.

TAM: I wis up the cash and carry fur, eh . . .

BOTH: Navid. You anglin' fur an invite an' aw?

TAM: Naw, just bein' neighbourly. Aye. I've got tae be at that weddin'. I cannae miss it. Aw that lovely Indian grub.

VICTOR: Oh, by the way, Wullie Macintosh is deid.

TAM: Who?

THEY MIME THE SPLAT.

TAM: Oh, aye. Here, that bastard's got a deep-fat fryer belongin' tae me.

JACK: Did that miserable auld prick huv anythin' o' his ain?

VICTOR: Borrowin' bastard. Anyway. They're burnin' him the morra.

JACK: Right, Tam, what's in the van?

TAM: Ach, the lot. Can I interest you in a couple of bottles of Lucozade?

VICTOR: Naw.

TAM: Gaun. Couple of bottles of Lucozade! Take the edge aff it.

JACK: Ach, I don't like . . .

TAM: Come on – it's right here.

BOTH: Right. OK.

TAM HANDS OVER TWO BOTTLES.

TAM: There ye are. Two pound forty.

VICTOR: You rippin' the piss?

JACK: That's what it costs in the shop.

TAM: I'm savin' ye a walk! Two pound forty.

THERE'S A PAUSE.

TAM: Fine.

TAM TAKES THE BOTTLES BACK, RIPS OPEN A MARS BAR AND STARTS EATING IT.

TAM: I cannae go gein' oot Navid's merchandise fur free – he'll huv ma guts fur garters come the stocktake! Gotta focus! Gotta think aboot that invite!

TAM SCREECHES AWAY.

7. EXT. DALDOWIE CREMATORIUM. DAY.

A MAN IS WHISPERING TO VICTOR, WHO NODS.

VICTOR: Nae danger, Kenny. We'll sort that fur ye.

JACK: What wis he wantin'?

VICTOR: (writing something down) He wants us to retrieve a pair of wally dugs that Wullie hoovered aff him in, get this, 1937.

JACK: Jesus. '37 . . .
there's me, nine,
stonnin' ootside the
Gaumont, waitin' tae
see *The Wizard of
Oz*, and that bastard
Wullie wis poncin'
even back then.

VICTOR: This list is gettin'
stupit.

THE MOURNERS FILE PAST A PRIEST. EACH ONE IS THANKING HIM FOR THE SERVICE. THERE'S ISA, TAM, WINSTON AND FINALLY JACK AND VICTOR.

JACK: Lovely. Very fitting. Very apt.

VICTOR: Very apt indeed – nice and personal.

THEY STEP FORWARD OUT OF THE PRIEST'S EARSHOT.

JACK: Well, that was a shower of shite.

VICTOR: It never ceases tae amaze me how wrang these tits get it. Fine upstanding member of the community. My arse. He's never met Wullie in his bloody life.

JACK: And he's stonnin' there spoutin' that pish as if he wis his best pal.

             THE PRIEST LEANS BACK IN.

PRIEST: Will you be joining us for the meal?

BOTH: I think so, Father. That
             would be lovely.

             AS THEY SPEAK,
             NAVID'S VAN ROLLS
             INTO THE FRAME
             WITH TAM DRIVING.
             WINSTON HOPS OUT
             THE PASSENGER
             SIDE AND SIDLES UP.

WINSTON: What would be lovely?

VICTOR: We've been invited up for some free scr . . . eh, a meal. Kindly.

JACK: Steak pie probably.

WINSTON: Sorry, Father – we've got a prior engagement.

JACK: Eh?

WINSTON: We're going to pay our respects to Wullie privately.

             WINSTON SURREPTITIOUSLY DANGLES A KEY BEHIND AN
             OPEN HAND TO REMIND JACK AND VICTOR.

PRIEST: Oh, really? (becoming chatty) Where are you off to?

JACK: Ye see, Faither, Wullie was an awfy tapper. And his hoose is
             cram packed full of stuff that isnae his. While everyone's down
             here payin' their
             respects that gies us
             the chance to fire . . .

             WINSTON STEPS
             ROUND, SHIELDING
             JACK FROM THE
             PRIEST. HE GIVES
             JACK A BRUTAL
             SHARP JAB TO THE

STOMACH. JACK IS WINDED AND IMMEDIATELY SHUTS UP. VICTOR AND WINSTON TAKE AN ARM EACH AND WALK HIM TO THE VAN. THE PRIEST GOES BACK TO THANKING OTHER MOURNERS.

8. EXT. WULLIE'S HOUSE. DAY.

JACK, VICTOR, WINSTON AND TAM STAND ON THE DOORSTEP, SOLEMNLY SURVEYING THE SCENE. THERE ARE NINETEEN BOTTLES OF UNOPENED MILK AND A LETTER BOX JAMMED TO THE GUNNELS WITH NEWSPAPERS.

JACK: (after a few moments' silence) Victor.

VICTOR: Aye, Jack.

JACK: Dinnae let this happen tae me. Aw piled up and naebody checkin' on ye.

VICTOR: That would never happen, Jack. For I would cancel my own milk order and simply take yours – free milk.

JACK: (indignantly) Dead man's milk!

VICTOR: Best of gear. And I would continue to do so until the relevant authorities corrected their error.

WINSTON AND TAM
GO INTO A KINK. A
SHIFTLESS YOUNG
NED OF A POSTMAN
SIDLES UP.

POSTIE: 'Scuse me, muckers. Mind yer backs.

HE SHOVES HIS WAY
THROUGH AND STRUGGLES TO CRAM A FISTFUL OF LETTERS INTO THE LETTER BOX.

JACK: What's you name, son?

POSTIE: Chris.

JACK: Chris. Caring Chris. Caring Chris the Community Postman. Take a
             second, Chris, and tell us all what you see wrang wi' this scene.

POSTIE: Shitload o' milk.

VICTOR: And what does that tell you about the occupant of this property?

POSTIE: No' intae milk.

JACK: No' intae milk . . . Observe the bottles closest to the door.

             JACK POPS THE LID OFF THE BOTTLE AND TURNS IT UPSIDE
             DOWN.

JACK: No longer milk but, in fact, cheese.

TAM: Notice the stuffed letter box. It would appear that the occupant is
             (mimicking the postman) no' intae letters.

WINSTON: (also mimicking) Or papers or such.

JACK: Now, you dim-witted prick, what is wrang wi' the man that lives here.

             THERE IS A LONG PAUSE. AFTER WHAT SEEMS LIKE
             FOREVER, THE POSTIE PIPES UP.

POSTIE: 'Se deid?

             THE MEN BREAK
             INTO VERY POLITE
             QUIET APPLAUSE
             BEFORE TURNING
             ON THE POSTIE.
             THEY KNOCK HIS
             HAT OFF, KICK HIS
             ARSE AND SHOVE
             HIM DOWN THE
             PATH, INSULTING
             HIM AS HE GOES.

POSTIE: 'Is is interferin' wi' Her
             Majesty's post!

ALL: Gaun, get lost! Piss
             off, Einstein! Sher-
             lock! Away ya go!

TAM: Right, Lads. Check wur watches. We've got one hour before Navid realises his van's missin'.

VICTOR: Who's got the list?

JACK: Right here.

      THEY ALL PILE INTO WULLIE'S FLAT.

9. INT. WULLIE'S HOUSE. DAY.

      WINSTON STANDS SURVEYING A ROPEY PAINTING OF THE TAJ MAHAL. TAM AND JACK PASS. JACK CARRIES A WOODEN TOILET PAN SEAT, TAM A LAMPSHADE.

JACK: Aye. Four slices at a time. That's more toast than ye need!

TAM: (bored out his tits and trying to get away) Aye, ye're right enough, Jack.

JACK: What are ye lookin' at?

      AS JACK LOOKS AT THE PAINTING, TAM GETS AWAY.

JACK: That's shite.

WINSTON: Yes, it is shite. But this is going to be my passport to the weddin'.

JACK: Eh?

WINSTON: I wis never that keen on it. Wullie hoached it aff me twenty-odd year ago. Now I'm claiming it back and I'm gonnie gie it to Navid. He's Taj Mahal daft. He'll be that grateful, I'll find masel' wan invite up.

JACK: (heading outside) Away ye go, ya fly bastard.

10. EXT. BY THE VAN. DAY.

VICTOR STANDS AT THE BACK OF THE VAN, HE CHECKS HIS
LIST. JACK IS CARRYING A GRAVY BOAT.

VICTOR: Gravy boat. Betty Curran. Do you remember yet what you lent 'im?

JACK: Naw. It's driving me aff ma nut.

VICTOR WRITES OUT BETTY CURRAN ON A POST-IT AND
STICKS IT ON. HE THROWS THE GRAVY BOAT ON TO THE
PILE. THE VAN IS STUFFED. POST-ITS CAN BE SEEN ON
EVERYTHING.

VICTOR: Ye better hurry up, just the bedroom now and that's us.

11. INT. BEDROOM IN WULLIE'S HOUSE. DAY.

WE SEE THE BEDROOM DOOR OPENING FROM THE INSIDE.
THE OLD MEN FILE IN. JACK TURNS TO FACE VICTOR AND
TAM.

JACK: That's what it was.

WE CUT ROUND TO
SEE VICTOR AND
TAM STANDING IN
FRONT OF A
HORRIBLE,
GRIMACING STUFFED
RACOON.

JACK: That's what I lent him.

WINSTON: Ye forgot ye lent him a bloody . . . What is it?

JACK: It's a racoon – all the way fae Canada . . . Ma Fiona sent it tae me.
            Jean hated it so I wis only too happy to lend it tae Wullie. It's a belter,
            intit?

WINSTON: Aye, a belter of a racoon right enough. Bit manky, but.

WINSTON TAPS IT. STOOR JUMPS OFF IT.

TAM: He husnae looked efter it well.

            TAM HITS IT. MORE STOOR FLIES UP.

JACK: Aye, I know – let's phone the RSPCA. It'll hoover up smashin'. Let's
            get it on the van.

12. EXT. NAVID'S SHOP. DAY.

            JACK AND VICTOR LOOK INTO THE WINDOW OF THE SHOP,
            JUST IN TIME TO SEE NAVID STEPPING DOWN A LADDER. HE
            HAS HUNG HIS TAJ MAHAL PAINTING. THEY ENTER THE SHOP.

13. INT. NAVID'S SHOP. DAY.

NAVID: 'Ere ye are, Alec. The invite is for you and your wife.

COPPER: Magic, Navid. That's fantastic.

            THE COPPER OPENS THE ENVELOPE. HIS FACE LIGHTS UP
            GOLD. WE HEAR THE SITAR MUSIC. HE EXITS.

NAVID: See and keep they wee neds fae hingin' aboot outside the shop.

COPPER: I will do. Thanks
            again, Navid.

NAVID: Hello, gentlemen.
            Lovely big fella, that.
            How do you like my
            new painting?

BOTH: Rare. Taj Mahal, eh?
            Quite something.

VICTOR: (to Meena sitting on a milk crate) Just saying it's a lovely paintin'
            Navid's got there.

            WE HEAR A GRUNT FROM BEHIND THE PAPER SHE'S READING.

NAVID: Don't ask her anything. Ignorant bastard. She thought the Sistine
            Chapel was in the Gorbals. What can I do you for?

JACK: Eh. Um. Fry's Cream.

VICTOR: Em. Um. I'll take a . . . pack of . . . Bubbalicious.

NAVID: Fry's Cream. Bubbalicious. Op. I'm glad you came in.

            NAVID BENDS DOWN OUT OF SHOT TO PICK SOMETHING UP.

JACK: Here we go.

VICTOR: Steady.

            NAVID PLACES
            SOMETHING IN A
            NEWSPAPER,
            TITTERS AND POPS
            BACK UP.

NAVID: There ye go. *Racing Post*. Delivery boy's aff – his dug got kilt.

JACK: *Post*. 'Zat it?

VICTOR: That's wur whack, eh?

NAVID: Yes, gentlemen. That is your whack.

VICTOR: Right.

JACK: Fine. Charmin'.

            THEY LEAVE, HUFFILY. THERE ARE A FEW BEATS. AN OLD
            MAN WALKS UP TO THE COUNTER FROM THE BACK OF THE
            SHOP.

OLD MAN: Where de ye keep yer Special K, Navid?

            NAVID LOOKS LIKE
            HE HAS SEEN A
            GHOST.

NAVID: Wullie Macintosh!
            You're deid! You're
            deid!

WULLIE: No, I'm no'.

NAVID: Are, ye are. Everyone wis at yer funeral yesterday.

WULLIE: Navid, I'm no' deid. I wis in the hospital but I'm no' deid.

NAVID: Aye, ye are. Ye're deid. Isa.

ISA: (from behind an aisle) Aye.

NAVID: Sure he's deid.

ISA: Aye.

SHE IS ASHEN FACED BUT NOT AFRAID. SHE WALKS UP TO HIM.

ISA: We buried ye yesterday, Wullie. I wis so sorry tae hear of your passin'. But ye've goat tae move on. Ye cannae wander amongst the living. Your place is in the spirit world noo.

SHE HOLDS UP A CROSS FROM ROUND HER NECK.

ISA: Go fae here and rest.

WULLIE: It's no' rest I'm needin', Isa – it's a boax o' Special K.

NAVID: Isa – gie deid Wullie his Special K.

WULLIE: For the last time – I'm no' deid. Can a deid guy do this?

HE STARTS TO FIRE COLA BOTTLE SWEETIES INTO HIS MOUTH.

WULLIE: Eh? Can he?

NAVID: (pulling the sweetie box away) I believe you.

ISA THROWS HER ARMS ROUND HIM.

ISA: Wullie!

WHILE WULLIE IS HUGGING ISA, HE CLOCKS NAVID'S TAJ MAHAL PAINTING.

WULLIE: I've got that painting.

14. EXT. CLANSMAN. DAY.

JACK AND VICTOR ARE ABOUT TO ENTER THE PUB. THEY SEE WINSTON OFF ON THE HORIZON.

JACK: Winston! Winston!

IN THE DISTANCE, WINSTON OPENS SOMETHING. IT GLINTS GOLD IN THE SUN. JACK AND VICTOR ARE TEMPORARILY DAZZLED IN THE GLARE. THEY ENTER THE PUB.

15. INT. CLANSMAN. DAY.

JACK AND VICTOR APPROACH THE BAR.

JACK: What de ye make o' that bugger Navid?

VICTOR: He's an arsehole.

BOABBY: Look who it isnae . . .

JACK: Oh, that's fantastic patter, Boabby. Who are we no' the day? Prick.

VICTOR: Two lager, ya f . . . fanny.

BOABBY: Jesus Christ! What's the matter wi' youse two?

JACK: That bastard Navid. We havnae managed tae get invited to that weddin'.

BOABBY: Oh, really. That's
            sad. It would bring a
            tear to yer eye. Och.
            I'm away. (mock
            tears) Let me wipe
            them dry.

            BOABBY WIPES
            THEM WITH AN
            INVITE. JACK AND
            VICTOR CLOCK THIS. BOABBY OPENS THE INVITE. WE HEAR
            SITAR MUSIC.

JACK: You! You've tae get gaun and we've no'? You! The black-hearted
            bastard barman fae the Clansman. Well, that's just dandy.

            TAM IS FINISHING UP A DRINK.

TAM: That's me away, Boabby. Is it raining outside, boys?

JACK: Spittin'. How?

TAM: Must remember tae put oan ma hat!

            TAM PRODUCES AN
            INVITE. HE OPENS IT.
            A GLINT OF GOLD
            FLASHES ACROSS
            HIS FACE. WE HEAR
            SITAR MUSIC. HE
            WINKS AT JACK AND
            VICTOR AND SALLIES
            OUT THE DOOR.

            THE PUB IS IN
            HYSTERICS. OUT OF THE DUST, A WEE COUPLE COME
            FORWARD AND STAND IN FRONT OF JACK AND VICTOR. THEY
            ARE SERIOUS AND, AS THEY SPEAK, THE PUB FALLS QUIET.

WOMAN: Jack. Victor. You'd be more than welcome to take our invites.

BOTH: Eh?

            THE MAN PLACES A SOMBRE ARM AROUND THE WOMAN.

WOMAN: Ma sister Mary goes in for a bypass the night before. I'll be up tae high doh. We just wouldnae enjoy it, would we, Charlie?

CHARLIE NODS IN AGREEMENT.

VICTOR: We couldnae, hen.

JACK: No, ye're alright, darlin'.

WOMAN: Take them. It's no' oor kind of thing anyway. Singin' and dancin'. All
            that rich food. It's no' for us. On ye go.

SHE OFFERS THE
INVITES ONCE MORE.
JACK AND VICTOR
EXCHANGE A LOOK.
THEY REACH FOR
THE INVITES AND
THE WOMAN
WITHDRAWS THEM.

WOMAN: That wis a lot of made-up pish. Away, ye pair of silly auld bastards!
            De ye think we'd miss a night oot like that?

THE PUB GOES INTO
A KINK. JACK AND
VICTOR LOSE THE
RAG AT THE PUB.

JACK: Do you think it's funny,
            uh? Eh?

VICTOR: Well, get it up yis.
            Me and my pal Jack
            wouldnae even go now if we were asked. The humiliation we've
            hud tae endure.

HE WAVES THE
RACING POST. AN
INVITE FALLS OUT.
JACK AND VICTOR
FALL SILENT. THEY
EYE IT. THEY BOTH
MAKE A DIVE FOR IT
AND CLUNK HEADS
LIKE COCONUTS.
VICTOR GETS IT.

VICTOR: Victor. It says Victor. Back off.

HE OPENS IT. JACK STANDS PITIFULLY NEXT TO HIM.
VICTOR'S FACE IS BATHED WITH GOLD AS JACK SINKS INTO
THE SHADOW. SITAR MUSIC CAN BE HEARD.

VICTOR: Oh, Mummy, Daddy. It's beautiful. Just beautiful.

JACK: Does it say Victor and friend?

VICTOR: Let me see now.

VICTOR OPENS IT AGAIN. MORE SITAR MUSIC. HE SPEED-
READS IT IN A MUMBLING STYLE.

VICTOR: No.

VICTOR WALKS OVER TO BOABBY WHO OFFERS HIS HAND.

VICTOR: What ye wearin', Boabby boy? Ye wearin' a suit?

BOABBY: Aye.

BOABBY GETS VICTOR A WHISKY.

WE SEE JACK STAND ALONE IN THE MIDDLE OF THE PUB
WHILE ALL AROUND HIM, PEOPLE ENTHUSE ABOUT THE
UPCOMING WEDDING. JACK GOES TO LEAVE. THE PUB DOOR
BURSTS OPEN. IT'S PETE THE JAKEY.

PETE: I'm gaun tae the weddin'! I'm gaun!

WE SEE JACK LEAVE ON THE FINAL INSULT. NO SOONER HAS
HE GONE THAN HE RETURNS AGAIN.

JACK: Wait a minute. Nae disrespect, Pete, but you are a pish-stained
            rancid tramp. How, in the name of Christ, do you get an invite?
            Lemme see that.

JACK SNATCHES THE INVITE FROM PETE.

JACK: Says Jack on this.

PETE: Aye. Um. My name's Jack.

JACK: Your name's Pete.

PETE: U've aye been cried Jack. It's a nickname.

JACK: Fur what?

PETE: Fur Pete. Jack's short for Pete. I found it.

VICTOR: Jack! It must huv fallen oot ma *Racin' Post*! That's your invite.

A SHORT
WRESTLING MATCH
RESULTS IN JACK
GETTING THE INVITE
AWAY FROM PETE.
JACK SHOVES PETE
OUT THE PUB.

JACK: Gaun oot. Ya thievin'
            smelly bastard!

JACK CLENCHES HIS FIST IN VICTORY.

16. INT. WEDDING RECEPTION. DAY.

JACK, VICTOR, ISA, ET AL. ARRIVE IN THE FOYER.

JACK: Wait a bloody minute, Isa, we were at his funeral!!

ISA: Naw, we wurnae. He wis in the hospital, right . . .

UNDERNEATH THIS LINE, WE CUT TO A NURSE WALKING
TOWARDS WULLIE IN A HOSPITAL BED.

NURSE: Wullie Macintosh?

WULLIE AND THE
MAN IN THE NEXT
BED BOTH LOOK UP.

BOTH: Aye?

BOTH: (smiling and looking at
            each other) Eh?

CUT BACK TO ISA AND JACK AND VICTOR.

VICTOR: Jesus! So, eh, two . . . It wis . . . Jesus.

ISA: Aye!

JACK: Wullie might as well be deid. We've emptied his hoose!

VICTOR: I suppose that means we have to go roon everybody and get all that stuff back . . .

JACK: . . . that didnae belang tae him . . .

VICTOR: . . . and gie it back?

BOTH: Naw.

VICTOR: Right. Youse lot get a seat and we'll get them in.

            JACK AND VICTOR HEAD TO THE BAR. THEY PASS A COUPLE OF TABLES. THEY NOD EXCITEDLY TO FELLOW GUESTS MOST OF WHOM ARE ASIAN.

JACK: A cannae believe we're here, Victor. I'm gonnie get pished.

VICTOR: Aye. Me and awe. I'll need tae be wheeled hame in a barra. Will ye take something to eat?

JACK: Are ye daft? I'm gonnie eat ma weight. Line ma stomach. Means ye kin drink more!

            THEY STROLL UP TO THE BAR. THEY'RE FACED WITH CLOSED SHUTTERS.

VICTOR: What's this?

JACK: Shut?

            NAVID STROLLS OVER.

NAVID: Jack, Victor. Good to see you! Thank you for coming.

JACK: Aye, aye. Where's the drink?

NAVID: Nae drink at a Muslim wedding, Jack.

VICTOR: Nae drink?

NAVID: It's a bastard, intit? Ye'll get a soft drink at the crush bar.

JACK: Now, Navid, yer daughter's present will be alang presently.

VICTOR: Very good, Jack. Present presently.

              THEY ENJOY A CHUCKLE AT THEIR GAG.

              WINSTON STROLLS OVER IN FULL HIGHLAND DRESS.

JACK: Winston, look at you. Jesus!

VICTOR: Very smart indeed, Winston. Ye look like fell aff a shortbreed tin.

WINSTON: I enjoy a kilt. Comfy tae. Leaves yer tackle hingin' free and easy, ye
              know.

ISA: So, Winston, what
              does a true
              Scotsman keep
              under his kilt?

WINSTON: At a Muslim weddin'?

              WINSTON LIFTS HIS
              KILT TO REVEAL
              BOOZE.

WINSTON: What's everyone wantin'?

JACK: I'll take that wee miniature!

WINSTON: Shut it.

CLOSING MUSIC AND CREDITS, THEN:

17. INT. CLANSMAN. DAY.

              JACK, VICTOR, TAM AND WINSTON SIT AT A TABLE. JACK HAS
              A TOASTER OUT OF A BAG. EVERYONE IS BORED LISTENING
              TO JACK.

JACK: Eh? Eh? Four slices. Toasting concurrently.

VICTOR: Jack, put the toaster away. Let's huv wur pints, eh? Oh Jesus.

JACK: What?

VICTOR: Wullie Macintosh.

JACK: Shite. Hello, Wullie.

WULLIE: Lads.

WINSTON: (awkwardly) We hear ye're no' deid.

WULLIE: Aye.

WINSTON: Smashin'.

TAM: Back fae the deid. Ye must be chuffed.

WULLIE: Ma hoose wis tanned.

ALL: No. Oh, my! Really?

WULLIE: Best of it is, ma postie seen who dunnit.

ALL: Postie? Seen it? Good!

WULLIE: Get this. Four old guys.

ALL: Old men? At the rob? Burglers?

WULLIE: Took the lot. Cannae even make masel' a slice of toast in the morning.

VICTOR: We cannae have that, can we, Jack?

JACK: Eh? What?

VICTOR: Take this one. It's a four slicer.

WULLIE: I couldnae.

VICTOR: Don't be daft.

JACK: Wire in.

WULLIE: I'll just take a lane o' it, eh?

5. GAIRDEN.

This idea came out the blue. It seemed to us that to have a lovely wee garden up the top of the high flats would be great. The question was – how do we go about it? We meet yet another of Winston's neme-, um, nemesis's? Nemesii? Nemesiseseses. The two neds with the devil dog. Filming this episode was absolutely freezing as we started series two on 7 January 2002. The Christmas pudding and Ne'er Day cordial hadn't even settled and we were out at the Maryhill bandstand, filming this oaf of a dog sniffing our nuts. What fun.

Of course, Isa's traits come to the fore in this episode. She is at her nosy best and demonstrates to Winston that she is not above blackmail to find out what he is up to. Isa is played by Jane McCarry who we also met on *Pulp Video* and have been close to ever since.

She is a whizz at remembering dialogue and, on a few occasions when an episode would come in short, we would always write her an extra last minute scene because we couldn't be bothered learning a new scene ourselves!

We couldn't get permission from the council to build an actual garden atop a tower block so the whole set was recreated 5 feet off the ground on a hill in Nitshill. On the set, the camera was always placed low so as not to catch any trees and buildings on screen and that gave the illusion that we were up the high flats. (If you look closely, you can see one tree in the distance. That tree would have to be 250 feet high. Oh my God, read that back. It is so boring. Shall we take it out? Naaah. Leave it in. Some clown will find it interesting.)

Our favourite scene in this episode is where Jack and Victor discuss the various ways to deal with your Tunnock's Tea cake wrapper. If you have seen a run of *Still Game*, you can't fail to have noticed our obsession with Scottish biscuits and, for years now, we have been waiting for the call from Mr Tunnock inviting us to be his ambassadors. Was that the phone?

Ford and Greg

GAIRDEN.

1. EXT. PARK. DAY.

JACK AND VICTOR SETTLE ON A BENCH IN THEIR RUN DOWN, CRAPPY PARK. THEY ARE OPENING TUPPERWARE CONTAINERS AND PREPARING TWO CUPS FROM THEIR FLASK. EVENTUALLY THEY SETTLE. A BALL IS RATTLED OFF JACK'S HEAD.

VICTOR: Here, you! It says nae ball games there. Can ye no' read?

VOICE: (off) Shut up, ya auld dick!

JACK GOES TO TAKE A BITE OF HIS SANDWICH. TWO BIKES WHIZZ PAST STIRRING UP A LITTER WHIRLWIND.

JACK: I hate this park.

VICTOR: Aye, me an' aw.

VICTOR TAKES A BITE OF HIS SANDWICH.

VICTOR: Picnic in Bosnia.

JACK: Can you smell shite?

VICTOR: Naw.

JACK: I can smell shite.

JACK OPENS HIS PIECE TO INVESTIGATE.

VICTOR: (sarcastically) Oh, aye. Right enough. That's what I made this morning. Two pieces and shite.

JACK TAKES A SIP FROM HIS CUP.

VICTOR: An' that's a flask o' piss to go wi' them.

JACK: Well, I'm no' imaginin' it 'cause I can definitely smell shite.

JACK CLOCKS HIS
SHOE. IT IS CAKED
IN AN ALMIGHTY
TURD. WITH GREAT
EFFORT HE PLACES
HIS FOOT RIGHT
UNDER VICTOR'S
NOSE. VICTOR
LOSES HIS APPETITE
AND THROWS HIS
SANDWICH IN THE GARBAGE.

JACK: Oh. Brand new an' aw – fresh oot the station.

VICTOR: That's aw people use this park fur noo. They bring their dugs doon
             tae empty their guts.

             JACK GETS OFF THE BENCH AND BEGINS TO WIPE HIS SHOE
             ON THE GRASS BEHIND IT.

JACK: It used to be all go in this park, remember?

VICTOR: Aye.

JACK: Bandstand. Swings. Sandpit. (pointing to a derelict shed) Ye used
             tae get a poky hat ootae there.

VICTOR: Somebody should come doon here wi' a camera. And catch these
             lazy bastarts letting their dugs dae their manky business aw over
             the place.

JACK: 'Here, you!' I'd say. 'Get that picked up! Get that muck disposed of!'

VICTOR: Aye!

             A SCARY TATTOOED THUG ENTERS SHOT. HE HAS AN
             ENORMOUS ROTTWEILER IN TOW AND A SKINNY WEEDY
             SNEERY PAL. THE DUG SQUATS AND PRODUCES AN
             ALMIGHTY SHITE PILE RIGHT BETWEEN THE TWO OLD MEN.
             THIS EVENT TAKES PLACE IN COMPLETE SILENCE.

TATTOOED MAN:
             That annoys you, din't it?

JACK: What?

TATTOOED MAN:
         Ma dug – daein a turd – right in the park.

VICTOR: Naw.

JACK: Not at all. Your park,
            ma park – wire in.

TATTOOED MAN:
            You think I should pick
            that up din't ye?

VICTOR: Naw.

TATTOOED MAN:
         Aye, ye dae. But I'm no' gonnie. I'm just leavin' it where it is.

JACK: Smashin'.

TATTOOED MAN:
         I'n't that right, Kaiser?

         KAISER GOES OVER AND BURIES HIS HEAD IN JACK'S
         CROTCH.

JACK: Jesus.

VICTOR: Easy, Jack.

TATTOOED MAN:
         I could make youse pick it up, but.

WEEDY MAN:
         Thatswhattaedaemakethempickitup –
         honsawshitepititinthebin! hahahaha

JACK: I'm sure you could.

TATTOOED MAN:
         Right. 'Mon, Kaiser.

         THE MENACING MAN EXITS MENACINGLY WITH SNEERY PAL.

JACK: I hate this park.

VICTOR: Aye, me an' awe.

2. INT. FOYER OF OSPREY HEIGHTS. DAY.

> TAM AND JIMMY ARE BUSTLING INTO THE ELEVATOR WITH A
> HUGE POT PLANT, A BAG OF COMPOST AND A STACK OF
> WINDOW BOXES. JIMMY PRESSES THE LIFT BUTTON TO
> CLOSE THE DOOR. TAM STOPS HIM.

TAM: Woa, woa, woa. What aboot the bench?

JIMMY: Oh, Jesus, aye! Eh. We'll come back fur it.

> ISA HAS FOLLOWED A TRAIL OF COMPOST RIGHT TO THE LIFT
> DOOR.

ISA: Oh. What are youse two doin' in this block? You don't live up here. Are ye visitin' sumbdy? Is this compost? Will ye be tidying that up? I hope ye're gonnie move that bench! What is it yis are daein?

TAM: (counting the questions in his head before answering) Yes, yes, yes, yes and mind yer ain business, ya nosy cow.

3. INT. CLANSMAN. DAY.

> JACK AND VICTOR ENTER THE PUB.

BOABBY: Youse two have got nothin' tae dae aw day but watch telly. What wis the name of that horror film – 60s – big fella – that nearly got Frankenstein. The . . . eh . . .

JACK: Was it *Attack of the Lazy Bastard Barman*?

VICTOR: *Arsehole Barman fae the Swamp*?

JACK: *I Married the Dobber Barman fae the Clansman*?

VICTOR: Two pints.

BOABBY: I don't know why I don't bar you two.

VICTOR: 'Cause ye fancy us, ya big woofter.

JACK: So, when ye're finished eyeing wur arses, gonnie get us wur pints?

> WINSTON COMES INTO THE PUB. HE IS CARRYING A MID-

SIZED POTTED PLANT. HE EAVESDROPS ON JACK AND VICTOR. HE IS CHUCKLING AWAY TO HIMSELF AT WHAT HE HEARS.

VICTOR: If I was twenty years younger I would have booted that clown in the park intae the pond.

JACK: Aye. And I would huv shoved ma hon doon that dug's throat and ripped it's lungs oot. Eeer yar!

WINSTON: Easy, Tiger. Who's gettin' it noo?

VICTOR: Ach, some arsehole ned. Lordin' it doon at that park.

JACK: He's got wan o' thae devil dugs.

WINSTON: And you're gonnie take the dug oan? What was it? Rip it's lungs oot?

JACK: Aye. 'Fneed be.

WINSTON: Right-o. (turning to Victor) So what are you daein while this carnage is gaun on? Gein the ned a scheme bootin', no doubt?

VICTOR: Naturally.

WINSTON: Oh, what I wouldn't give to be ringside at that. A couple of frail old men against a big handy bastart and his wean-eatin' dug. In ma heart, I'd be cheerin' fur ma pals but, in ma pocket, would be a bettin' slip with ned and dug written oan it. Eejits.

JACK: Har bloody har.

VICTOR: Anyway, we'll no' be usin that park again. It's had it.

WINSTON: Quite right. I've no' been in it fur a fortnight.

JACK: What's wi' the plant?

WINSTON: That would be telling.

VICTOR: Aw, here we go.

WINSTON: Let's just say this (shaking the plant) is the reason I don't have to
            use said shitty park.

            JACK AND VICTOR LOOK PUZZLED. TWO OTHER OLD FELLAS
            ENTER CARRYING POT PLANTS.

WINSTON: (turning, he sees the pot-plant carrying men) Oh, very nice, Colin. A
            hosta – low maintanace – very rewarding to look at.

COLIN: What have you got?

WINSTON: Believe it or not, it's a eucalyptus tree – nice colour – nice scent –
            aromatic – forty feet in ten year, unmaintained.

JACK: Right, Percy, spill it.

WINSTON: No can do.

VICTOR: Get it telt.

WINSTON: I've said too much already – but ye're friends. When wis the last time
            you saw Tam or Eric or any of the boys in the shit park?

BOTH: Wee while . . . fornight or so . . .

WINSTON: (backing off with his pot plant) Aye. Well, think on, lads. Think on.

4. INT. NAVID'S SHOP. DAY.

            NAVID SITS WATCHING A PORTABLE BLACK-AND-WHITE TV. HE
            IS IDLY POPPING OUTERSPACERS INTO HIS MOUTH. AFTER
            HE'S HAD A COUPLE, MEENA PIPES UP IN PUNJABI.

MEENA: Stop eating the stock.

NAVID: Meena, it's my stock. I'll eat as many Outerspacers as I want. And,
            besides, I would have to eat for a thousand sleepless years to get
            my arse up to the size that yours is.

            ISA COMES IN FOR HER SHIFT. SHE APPROACHES THE
            COUNTER. SHE GIVES NAVID HER COAT AND HE GIVES HER A
            BRUSH AND DUST PAN.

ISA: Hello, Navid.

NAVID: Hello, Isa. So, tell me. What's the latest gossip from roon aboot? Bearing in mind you only have one minute 'cause *Columbo* is about to start.

ISA: (taking this as a challenge) One minute? Right. All the hooses in Samson Court are tae get double glazed fur nothing because the council's daein them noo that suggests tae me that ma block  might be next but Jeannie Maguire says no' tae haud ma breath 'cause that's three year they've been waitin'. That's Jeannie's boy workin' noo. He didnae want the job but she made him get it to pay for damage in the Laundromat. Thirty-eight and still livin' wi his ma. Terrible. Good news fur the bookie's brother. He'll no' lose his eye – it'll never look right but he'll get tae keep it. I caught Tam and Eric up to no good in the foyer liftin' benches an' plants and aw sorts I huvnae a clue whit's gaun on there but watch this space now, best fur last, ye mind of old Ronnie? Him that was on *Mastermind*? Aw. I'm out of time. There, yer programme startit.

NAVID TURNS TO THE TV. AFTER A FEW BEATS, HE TURNS BACK.

NAVID: Ye're OK, Isa. It's the episode wi' William Shatner. Lotta shite. (turning the telly off) What aboot Ronnie? What was his chosen subject again?

ISA: World War II boats. (conspiratorially) He lost by one point cause he passed on *Bismark*. I mean – *Bismark*.

NAVID: The most famous boat in the war. Tit.

ISA: He's in the loony bin.

NAVID: Eh?

ISA: Well, I say 'loony bin' – it's actually a home.

NAVID: Oh, Jesus. That's a shame. Another good customer down.

NAVID POPS ANOTHER OUTERSPACER IN HIS MOUTH. HE

NOTICES ISA EYEING UP THE SWEETS. HE BEGINS TO TAUNT
HER WITH THE TUB.

NAVID: Ooooh. Outerspacers. Look at ye. Yer mooth aw watery at the
            prospect. Wup! Wup. Take one.

MEENA: Stop eating the stock!

NAVID: (shooting Meena a dirty look) Meena says take a few!

5. INT. LANDING OF OSPREY HEIGHTS. NIGHT.

JACK AND VICTOR EMERGE ON TO THE LANDING FROM THEIR
RESPECTIVE FLATS. BOTH CARRY A PACKET OF BISCUITS.

VICTOR: Where are you gaun?

JACK: I'm comin' to you.

VICTOR: You're comin' tae me? I'm comin' tae you!

JACK: No. You were at me last night.

VICTOR: Are you sure? Did you no' come here? We watched that chef bollocks.

JACK: Was that no' the night before?

VICTOR: I don't know.

JACK: Well, you put them back and I'll come in to you and we'll eat these
            (waving his own pack of biscuits). What were ye bringin'?

VICTOR: Tunnock's Tea Cakes
            – the daddy of them
            all.

JACK: Accept no substitutes.
            Impressive. Well, we'll
            wire intae them as well.

VICTOR: No. That's no' how it
            works. These would
            get ate if I wis comin' tae you. What are you bringin?

JACK: Sad to announce, tea biscuits – apologies. C'mon. We'll just open yours.

VICTOR: Indeed we will not. These go back into the cupboard until such times as I come to you. Those are the rules.

JACK: Aye, I suppose so. Ye cannae come tae a man's house and eat his biscuits. That would be lawlessness. Anarchy! A downward spiral!

VICTOR: Shut up. We can huv wan each but we're no' finishin' them.

JACK: Result.

6. INT. FLAT. NIGHT.

WE SEE A COFFEE TABLE. ON IT SITS A FULL PACK OF TEA CAKES. ONE BY ONE THE BISCUITS FADE AND DISAPPEAR UNTIL THERE ARE NONE LEFT. JACK AND VICTOR SIT READING BOOKS.

JACK: They were smashin'. You wouldnae think ye could eat three.

VICTOR: That's 'cause you ate four.

JACK: Pish. I hud three. Fair share.

VICTOR: Four.

JACK: Nup.

VICTOR: (putting down his book) Would you like me to prove it?

JACK: Yes, I would enjoy that. Present yer case.

VICTOR: You do that really annoying thing of rolling up the foil intae a wee baw. You always do that. Like obsessive behaviour. (miming rolling the foil wrapper up into a ball) Now, if you observe

the remains, ye can clearly see four baws.

JACK: Aye, I'll accept that. Four, eh? Obsessive behaviour? Well what do you call this?

HE HOLDS UP TWO ALMOST IRONED FOILS.

JACK: Ye've got tension in yer anus. That's what they cry it.

VICTOR: (going back to his book) Thank you Sigmund.

JACK: They've got hospitals fur people that dae that. You're gonnie end up like Ronnie.

VICTOR: Jeez-o. Ronnie. What did ye make of that?

JACK: Accordin' tae Navid he wis runnin' aboot in his smalls smack bang in the middle of George Square. Daft.

VICTOR: Some come doon – fae *Mastermind* tae yer scants.

JACK: Every day he was in the library – we used tae see him, de ye mind?

VICTOR: Aye.

JACK: Bonin' up, book after book aboot war boats.

VICTOR: He knew everything there wis tae know. *The Hood*! *USS Indianapolis* . . .

JACK: U-boats – even knew the size of the guns tae the inch and what does he forget?

BOTH: *Bismark.*

JACK: Doolally bastart. Even Magnus was sniggering.

VICTOR: De ye think he just snapped then?

JACK: Aye. His boy came and got him. Put him in Balgarnock Home for
           the Elderly.

VICTOR: Jesus. That place is brutal. Semolina. That's aw they feed ye.

JACK: That's where they put Johnnie Muir. They call it The Terminus.

VICTOR: I would shoot masel' before I went in there – baith barrels.

JACK: Aye, what if you were too feeble-minded tae shoot yersel? Boof. Next
           thing ye know ye're sittin' there wi' a bib oan, spoon-fed semolina
           by a bastard nurse wi' a moustache who would rather see ye deid.

VICTOR: You'd be sittin' next tae me. Stinkin the place oot 'cause ye've shat
           yersel'. And ye've no' got the strength tae pick up yer skinny airm
           tae get anybody interested in cleanin' it up.

JACK: We'll need tae go see him.

VICTOR: Aye. The morra.

JACK: Aye. (pausing) Here, you could have fitted me up.

VICTOR: Eh?

JACK: When I went fur a piss. You could have easily took one of your nice
           flat wrappers and rolled it up into a baw and put it next to mine.

VICTOR: Good theory, Jack. Plausible. And it may have happened like that
           were it not for the fact that you are a greedy bastard.

           JACK BEGINS TO FLICK THE TINFOIL BALLS AT VICTOR.

VICTOR: Hey.

7. EXT. PARK. DAY.

           WINSTON STANDS AT A BUS STOP SITUATED AT THE PARK
           GATE. IN HIS ARMS HE HAS A BIN LINER WITH A BUSH
           HANGING OUT OF IT. THE TWO NEDS FROM EARLIER ARE
           EXITING THE PARK. THEY SPOT WINSTON AND BEGIN TO
           NOISE HIM UP.

TATTOOED MAN:
Here, you!

WINSTON: Me?

TATTOOED MAN:
Aye, you, auld yin.

WINSTON: What is it?

TATTOOED MAN:
What ye daein' wi' that bush? Are you George Bush?

WEEDY MAN:
HAHAHAHAHAHA –
George Bush. Ask
him if he's Kate Bush
an' aw, man. Ask him,
man, ask him.

TATTOOED MAN:
Shut up. Haw, are you
Kate Bush?

WINSTON: Aye, that's right. (under his breath) Half wits.

TATTOOED MAN:
Sing us a song, Kate Bush.

WEEDY MAN:
Aye, man. Totally make 'im sing, man . . .

WINSTON SPOTS THE BUS APPROACHING AND HE SEES HIS
OPPORTUNITY TO DISH BACK SOME ABUSE. THE BUS PULLS
UP. THE DOOR OPENS.

WINSTON: Haud on a second, son. See youse two, ya couple of pricks? If I
wisnae gettin' oan this bus I'd come over there and rip your airms
aff, ye wee tit, and batter the shite oot yer pal wi' them. You've ripped
the arse oot that park, ya perra inbred freak-show bastards! Look at
the two of you, eh? First time someone stands up tae ye, ye're struck
dumb and yer wee skinny arses collapse.

AS WINSTON IS RANTING, THE BUS DOORS CLOSE AND THE
BUS TAKES OFF. WHEN HE FINISHES, HE TURNS TO STEP ON
THE BUS BUT IT IS PULLING AWAY.

WINSTON: Oh, dear! (turning back to the neds) Only kiddin'!

WE CUT TO SEE THE NED UNLEASHING KAISER.

8. INT. PUB. DAY.

WE CUT TO SEE
WINSTON STANDING
SHAKING AT THE
BAR. HIS CLOTHES
ARE DISHEVELLED,
HIS SLEEVE AND
CROTCH ARE TORN.
HIS FACE IS
SCRATCHED.

WINSTON: . . . fifty – maybe sixty – pounds of devil dug on tap o me. Tearing at me. Tryin' tae eat me. I'm gein this bastard body blows. I must huv hit it forty times in the gut. Nuthin'. Didn't even wind it. Gnash, gnash, bite, snarl, rip. Then I've got my thumb in its eye. Aw I've done there is annoy it. I didnae go thirsty, but, 'cause I must've drunk aboot a pint of its slabbers.

ERIC: So how did ye get it aff ye?

WINSTON: I didnae. It clocked a wee dug and went and pumped it. Monster. It should be destroyed.

ERIC: Take a whisky, Winston. That'll settle ye.

WINSTON: Cheers, Eric.

ERIC: Not to worry, eh? (looking around to make sure no one else hears) I hear yer wee project's nearly finished.

WINSTON: That's right, Eric. We open tonight. Stick another half in there I'll make sure you get a good seat.

ERIC: Boabby!

9. EXT. BALGARNOCK HOME FOR THE ELDERLY. DAY.

VICTOR: It doesnae look that bad.

JACK: Aye, well kept. Lovely grounds.

VICTOR: No' so bad . . .

> AT THIS POINT, AN ANCIENT OLD MAN IN PYJAMAS AND GOONIE COMES UP.

OLD MAN: Smell ma fingers!

BOTH: Eh? Get yersel' tae fu . . . Get back

OLD MAN: Get them smelt! It's the good stuff!

JACK: Naw, ye're alright!

OLD MAN: Ye dunno whit ye're missin'!

> AT THIS POINT, A WELL-DRESSED MAN IN A WHITE COAT EMERGES. HE LOOKS LIKE AN ELDERLY DOCTOR.

DOCTOR: Hello, gentlemen. Can I help you?

VICTOR: Eh. We're here tae see wur pal – Ronnie Wilson.

DOCTOR: Oh, yes. Ronnie. I see ye've met Alex.

JACK: Aye. It's a sin that.

DOCTOR: This way then.

10. INT. BALGARNOCK. DAY.

> THE 'DOCTOR' LEADS JACK AND VICTOR ALONG A SUCCESSION OF CORRIDORS.

DOCTOR: It's a big old building this. Typical Victorian. They've actually done a fair bit of work to it over the years. It would have been quite literally bedlam in here 100 years ago. When I first came here, you'd be surprised at some of the cases. In here for years for as little as underage pregnancy, mild depression – of course we're talking  in the days before Prozac and what have you.

BOTH: Oh, aye.

DOCTOR: Anyway, that's us here.

HE STANDS AT A DOOR.

DOCTOR: If you could could just wait here a few moments . . .

JACK AND VICTOR STAND IDLE FOR A FEW SECONDS. THE 'DOCTOR' HAS HIS BACK TO CAMERA. THEY SLOWLY NOTICE THAT THE DOCTOR IS NOW MASTURBATING.

BOTH: Jesus! Ya filthy bastard!

THE DOCTOR SHUFFLES OFF LAUGHING. AT THIS POINT, WE HEAR AN OLD MAN SCREAM.

VOICE OVER:
            We're all going to die!

JACK CALMLY TURNS TO VICTOR. NODS AND LEGS IT. VICTOR GIVES CHASE.

VICTOR: Wait a minute.

JACK: No way, Jose. I'm outta here.

VICTOR: What aboot Ronnie?

JACK: Ronnie who?

VICTOR: Calm doon. Let's get a look at him. That's what we came for.

JACK: This place gies me the fear!

VICTOR: Op. There he is — in there!

JACK TURNS AWAY.

JACK: What's he daein? I'm feart tae look! Is he chuggin' 'issel'? Acting daft? Is he done up like a wummin?

VICTOR: No, he looks fine!

VICTOR TAPS THE GLASS. RONNIE LOOKS UP AND SMILES AND GIVES A WEE WAVE.

11. INT. TOP FLOOR LANDING. DAY.

WINSTON IS OPENING A PADLOCKED DOOR. AS HE DOES SO, HE SENSES A PRESENCE BEHIND HIM. HE LOOKS ROUND IN TIME TO SEE A DOOR DOWN TO THE TOP FLAT FLOOR CLOSING. THINKING HE'S BEEN CAUGHT, HE PADS DOWN THE STAIRS AND ON TO THE LANDING. HE SCANS ROUND THE LANDING. IT IS EMPTY. HE BREATHS A SIGH OF RELIEF, HIS SECRET IS SAFE. HE TURNS ROUND TO COME FACE TO FACE WITH ISA WHO MOPS INNOCENTLY. HE IS STARTLED.

WINSTON: Isa, ya bastard!

ISA: Hello, Winston.

WINSTON: What are you daein up here?

ISA: Mopping the landing.

WINSTON: Moppin' it fur who?

ISA QUICKLY CLOCKS THE NEAREST DOORPLATE.

ISA: Mr Sinclair.

WINSTON: Ye're aye helping oot, int ye? Daein' wee turns . . .

           SHE NODS SWEETLY.

WINSTON: That's how ye keep on tap of everybody's business, intit?

           SHE NODS AGAIN SMUGLY.

ISA: What's your business, Winston?

WINSTON: How de ye mean?

ISA: What's in behind that door?

WINSTON: You'd love tae know what's behind that door . . .

           ISA NODS.

WINSTON: It's killin' you not to know what's behind that door.

ISA: Winston, (looking about to make sure no one's listening) cards on
           the table. I'm a nosy bastard. I cannae no know whit's behind that
           door.

           SHE SHRUGS AS IF TO SAY 'SO THERE YOU ARE. HELP ME
           OUT HERE.'

WINSTON: (looking down at her message bag) Isa, see if you were to go intae
           yer bag and pull oot a Colt .45 and jam it in ma ear . . . I still wouldnae
           tell ye. Ye'd just huv tae shoot me.

           WE FOLLOW ISA'S HAND INTO HER BAG. IT EMERGES
           HOLDING A DINKY MOBILE PHONE.

WINSTON: What's that?

ISA: This is ma mobile
           phone. Ma son Colin
           bought it for me – in
           case I should take a
           fall or that. Ye know –
           emergencies. I don't
           even have tae dial his
           number. I press this.

Phonebook. C. Colin comes up. Oh. Craiglang library. Caretaker. Dear. They're so fiddly. I've made that mistake a few times. I've meant tae call Colin (her smile drops to deadpan) and ended up talking tae the caretaker.

IN AN INSTANT, WINSTON IS CRUSHED BEYOND REPAIR. DEFEATED. HE COMPOSES HIMSELF.

WINSTON: Isa, I'll take you through the door. Do you PROMISE not to divulge to any living soul what you are about to see?

ISA HESITATES.

WINSTON: (sternly) Isa . . .

ISA: I promise.

WINSTON: Then come with me.

WE CUT TO THE PADLOCK BEING OPENED. ISA GRABS THE DOOR HANDLE. THE SUSPENSE IS KILLING HER. WINSTON GRABS HER HAND.

WINSTON: Isa, not a word, now – tae anybody.

ISA: Not a word – tae anybody . . .

WINSTON THROWS OPEN THE DOOR. WE ONLY SEE ISA'S FACE. SHE CANNOT BELIEVE WHAT SHE IS SEEING. SHE BEGINS TO MENTALLY DISSOLVE. IT'S ALL TOO MUCH. SHE TURNS ON HER HEELS AND RUNS DOWN THE STAIR. WINSTON GIVES CHASE. SHE IS FRANTICALLY PRESSING THE LIFT BUTTON.

WINSTON: Isa! Isa!

ISA: It's too good! It's too good! People huv tae know!!!!

WINSTON PUTS HER
IN A HEADLOCK.

WINSTON: Isa! You promised!
Not a word! Tae
anybody! They'll take
it aff us! Promise!

ISA: I promise! Ye're
chokin' me! Let go!

WINSTON: Only if you don't tell!

ISA: I wullnae!

WINSTON SLOWLY LETS GO. ISA RUBS HER NECK AND
STRAIGHTENS HERSELF OUT. AFTER A BEAT, SHE LOSES IT
AGAIN AND BEGINS FRANTICALLY HITTING THE BUTTON
AGAIN.

WINSTON: (grabbing her in a headlock again) Aah ahaha!

12. INT. BALGARNOCK. DAY.

JACK AND VICTOR SIT WITH RONNIE AT A TABLE IN A DAY
ROOM. IN WING-BACK HOSPITAL CHAIRS, OTHER PATIENTS
SIT ABOUT SLOBBERING.

VICTOR: Ye look fine, Ronnie.

JACK: I must say masel', you look alright . . .

RONNIE: Course I look aright. There's heehaw wrang wi' me!

VICTOR: With all due respect, Ronnie. They'll aw be sayin' that in here –
'Nuthin' wrang wi' me! Lemme oot!'

RONNIE: Look, you two. I'm fine. I hud one goofy turn in George Square . . .

JACK: A goofy turn? We're no' talkin' aboot feelin' dizzy. Ye were doon tae
yer scants shoutin' and bawlin' like a daftie outside the City
Chambers!

RONNIE: I know. I'll tell ye what happened. I bought a magazine ootae WH Smith's and a pie ootae Gregg's. I thought I'll plonk masel' outside on George Square and have a wee read. I'm readin' an article  aboot pensioners that up sticks and go abroad and I doze off. I don't know how long I was asleep fur. A minute, an hour, I dunno. But next thing I know, I wake up and I'm ten year old, on a beach. It's roastin'. I'm telling ye. It didnae seem like a dream or anything. It wis real tae me. So, I've whipped the claes aff and I'm runnin aboot. I gets lifted and I didnae come tae till I'm in the back of the paddy wagon and I'm sayin', 'I'm alright!' Two hours later, ma Norman signs me in here. Bastard.

JACK: And ye're alright noo?

RONNIE: I'm fine. Really.

JACK: He certainly seems fine tae me. Does he seem fine tae you, Victor?

VICTOR: (after a suspicious pause) Which boat during World War II was sunk aff the coast of . . .

RONNIE: *Bismark.* Don't start! That doesnae prove anything! Let me ask you a question – how many Jap Zeros struck the *Cornelius* on July 27th 1944?

JACK: Ooooh. I don't know – now ye're askin' . . . Do you know?

VICTOR: I'd be guessin'. Four?

JACK: Four's a lot.

            JACK AND VICTOR TURN THEIR CHAIRS INWARD AND CONFER.

JACK: I'd say three. Mebbe two. Say two . . .

VICTOR: We're sayin' . . .

RONNIE: Never mind whit ye're sayin'. It wis fourteen. You didnae know that. Who's the daftie noo?

JACK: Jeezo. Bang, bang, bang, bang, bang, bang, bang, bang – ye'd think they would huv phoned somebody efter the first two or three.

VICTOR: Naw. They were fly. They always took out the communications first.

JACK: Aye. Fly bastards.

RONNIE: Listen tae this – the perra youse should be in here no' me.

VICTOR: Can ye no' sign yersel' oot?

RONNIE: No. It's got to be Norman that does it. He's ma only next of kin.

JACK: Well, where is he?

RONNIE: Norwich. And says he cannae get up for two weeks.

VICTOR: Two weeks?

RONNIE: Aye. I'm tellin' ye, boys, if I'm in here for another two hours I'll be as doolally as aw these other bastards.

          JACK AND VICTOR EXCHANGE A LOOK OF RESOLVE.

13. INT. LANDING. DAY.

          WE SEE ISA TEARING OUT OF A LIFT. SHE'S OUT OF BREATH. SHE RINGS A DOORBELL. AN OLD WOMAN ANSWERS.

ISA: Sadie. Thank God ye're in.

SADIE: (monotone, strangely vague) Hello, Isaaa . . .

ISA: You will never guess what Winston showed me . . .

SADIE: Whaat did Winston show you?

          ISA EYES SADIE. SHE SUSPECTS ALL IS NOT RIGHT.

SUDDENLY THE
DOOR WHIPS OPEN.
WINSTON STANDS
NEXT TO SADIE. HE
IS FURIOUS.

WINSTON: I knew you couldnae keep quiet! I knew this would be your first port of call – runnin' straight roon tae yer best pal. (Putting on a high voice) 'Sadie, you'll never guess what Winston's showed me!' You slabber cabbage bastard!!! C'mere!

WINSTON HEADLOCKS ISA AGAIN

WINSTON: Promise! Promise!

ISA: (choking) It's a weakness! I cannae help masel'!

14. INT. BALGARNOCK. DAY.

NURSE: So you're his brothers.

JACK: That's right. We're both the next of kins.

VICTOR: We've come fae abroad.

NURSE: Oh, really? Where?

BOTH: Canada/Australia.

VICTOR: Kinda Australia.

JACK: New Zealand.

VICTOR: Aye.

THE NURSE LOOKS AT JACK, THEN VICTOR, THEN RONNIE.
SHE SYMPATHISES.

NURSE: (against her better judgement) Riiight. Sign here, here and again here.

THEY BOTH GO TO SIGN HIM OUT.

VICTOR: Please, Jack.

JACK: Thank you, Victor. (signing) Dee dumm. Dee di . . . dee do.

VICTOR: Is that us then?

NURSE: (Smiling) Not unless you want to stay for yer tea.

ALL THREE SHARE THE NURSE'S JOKE.

JACK: What is fur tea?

VICTOR: (pushing Jack) Riiight.

JACK: Shovin. That wis easy enough, eh?

VICTOR: We're not out of here yet . . .

THE MASTURBATOR IS HEADING DOWN THE CORRIDOR
TOWARDS THEM.

DOCTOR: Hello, there. I see you found your friend. You must be Ronnie. Hello,
            Ronnie.

THE 'DOCTOR' STICKS HIS HAND OUT TO SHAKE IT. RONNIE
OFFERS HIS HAND. JACK INTERVENES.

JACK: Don't touch his hon.

15. INT. PUB. NIGHT.

TAM, ERIC AND WINSTON STAND AT THE BAR.

ERIC: What time will we have the unveiling?

TAM: Soon as we get these doon us.

WINSTON: Aye, but we'll need tae wait fur Jack and Victor. That'll be good tae.
            I've no' breathed a word to them. Get us a pint, Boabby.

BOABBY: Nae bother – hair of the dug, is it?

WINSTON: Very funny. I'd like to see how your wee skinny boady would huv faired under sixty pound o' devil dug. You would huv snapped like a twig!

BOABBY: No' me. Ye see the proper way to render an angry dug help-less is simply to insert a digit intae the dug's rectum. Boom. Bob's yer uncle – he releases his grip. Ye're a free man.

ERIC/TAM: Is that right?/Worth remembering, that.

WINSTON: And what do you dae efter ye've hud yer finger up its erse? Huv a wee cuddle? Lie there in the afterglow huvin' a post-coital cigarette? Plan the future? Puppies? Nice kennel fur the baith of yis? Away ye go, ya Queerhawk!

TAM AND ERIC DISSOLVE INTO LAUGHTER. BOABBY GOES AND CLEANS OPTICS.

ISA: (tapping Winston on the shoulder) I want a word with you.

WINSTON: Jesus, here we go.

ISA: I've just been sitting wi' Andy Begg, Jeannie Cassidy and Tommy Kinnoborough and they were delighted to inform me of what I've been told no' tae mention tae a soul . . . That makes me look like a halfwit. Like I'm in the dark! Like I know nothin'. Well, thank you. Thank you very much!

WINSTON: Look at you, Isa! Awe angry. Ragin! Calm doon.

TAM: Stick yer finger up her arse. That'll cool her beans.

ISA SLAPS TAM CLEAN IN THE GUB. HE ROCKS BACK. THE MEN FALL ABOUT.

JACK AND VICTOR ENTER WITH RONNIE.

ISA: Oh, Ronnie. How ye doin'?

VICTOR: Fine. And he could use a drink. So oot the way, Isa.

JACK: Usual fur us and it's Guinness you take, intit, Ronnie?

RONNIE: Aye. Lovely.

WINSTON: Guid tae huv ye back, Ronnie, boy.

              BOABBY BRINGS A PINT FOR WINSTON.

BOABBY: 1.80, Winston.

WINSTON: 1.80 – crazy prices. Ye'd huv tae be aff yer heid tae pay they prices.
              Mental. Nae offence, Ronnie. Right. Get these doon ye quick. We
              have somethin' tae show yis.

JACK/VICTOR:
              Eh?/Whit?

16. INT. TOP LANDING. NIGHT

              THE FIRST LIFT DOOR OPENS. JACK, VICTOR, ISA, WINSTON,
              RONNIE, TAM, ERIC AND TWO OTHERS PILE OUT.

JACK: That wis hairy. Nine bodies in there – ye're only meant tae huv eight.

VICTOR: That's a lot of shite. Ye can huv as many bodies as ye can squeeze
              in providing ye can get the door shut.

JACK: The plate in the lift said eight bodies max.

VICTOR: Are you coontin' yersel' as one?

JACK: Eh? Shut up. Ha ha. See how funny ye are when the lift is screamin
              doon the shaft at Mach 2 wi' a wee steel tail flappin' at the back o'
              it.

              DURING THIS LAST SPEECH, THE OTHER LIFT HAS ARRIVED
              WITH MORE PENSIONERS AND WINSTON IS ROUNDING THEM
              UP.

WINSTON: Right, everyone, as ye know the park doon the road is a shite-hole. (a few tuts) Sorry, ladies, but it is – an utter shitehole. And we'd rather no' huv anythin' tae dae wi' it. So, with great effort, a hardy band

teamed together and worked tirelessly to give you the new solution for rest and safe recreation for the over sixty-fives of Craiglang. Follow me, to a new dawn.

17. EXT. ROOF. NIGHT

THE DOOR OPENS. WINSTON HOLDS IT AS THEY ALL FILE OUT. WE CUT TO SEE A PERFECTLY RECONSTRUCTED PARKLET.

WINSTON GOES TO A SWITCH. HE HITS IT WITH A FLOURISH. A SET OF OLD-FASHIONED PARK LIGHTS COME ON.

WINSTON: Welcome to High Park.

JACK: Jesus.

VICTOR: It's beautiful.

ALL THE OTHER PENSIONERS BEGIN TO MILL AROUND THE AREA. THERE'S GRASS, A WINDY PATH AND A SIGN READING:

NAE BALL GAMES
NAE LITTERING
NAE BIKES
NAE NEDS
NAE BASTARD DEVIL
DUGS

WINSTON: Fantastic, eh?

JACK: Is that sausages I smell?

           AN OLD MAN IS GRILLING SAUSAGES ON A BARBECUE. HE
           WAVES OVER.

WINSTON: Indeed it is. Let me paint ye a wee picture. Roll and sausage. Yer
           paper. Sit on the bench there and, if you want, feed the duck.

           CUT TO A SINGLE DUCK SWIMMING IN A BLOW UP PADDLING
           POOL.

           THE THREE OF THEM
           MILL OVER TO THE
           BARBECUE.

VICTOR: Is the park just for
           night time, annat?

WINSTON: Day or night. Any time
           it all gets too much,
           just come up here.

JACK: Well done, Winston. Well done!

ISA: (off) Jack! Victor!

           JACK AND VICTOR
           LOOK ROUND.
           RONNIE STANDS IN
           HIS SCANTS IN A
           FLOWER BED –
           CLEARLY BONKERS.

RONNIE: A park. First a beach,
           noo a park! A sky
           park! A park in the
           sky!

CLOSING MUSIC AND CREDITS, THEN:

JACK AND VICTOR ARE IN THE SKY PARK. THEY SIT ON THE PARK BENCH.

JACK: Oh, this is rare. No' huvin tae watch yer back . . .

VICTOR: Nae kids on skateboards takin' the toes aff ye . . .

JACK: Nae dug mess – Christ, ye could practically come up here in yer slippers.

VICTOR POINTS TO HIS FEET. HE IS WEARING SLIPPERS.

JACK: Jeez-o. I'll dae that the morra. Huv ye fed the duck?

VICTOR: Aye. Hof a loaf the wee bugger ate . . .

AN OLD COUPLE APPROACH.

OLD MAN: Can we get a seat?

JACK: We've got it till hof three – ten minutes tae go.

VICTOR: Ach, c'mon. We've sat here long enough. Let them get a shot . . .

OLD MAN: Thank you.

BOTH: Nae bother/Ye're welcome.

SUDDENLY THE DOOR TO THE ROOF SLAMS OPEN. THERE STANDS THE TATTOOED MAN, HIS PAL AND THE DEVIL DUG.

TATTOOED MAN:
Quality. A park up in the air.

WEEDY MAN:
Aye, quality, man. A high up park up high, nae way, man – nae way.

VICTOR: Here, you. You've nae business being up here.

JACK: You've got the park doon the way.

TATTOOED MAN:

I'm no' wantin' that park. It's full of dug shite. I'm gonnie start comin' here noo.

WINSTON MARCHES OVER WITH A BAMBOO STICK. HE PRODS IT IN THE TATTOOED MAN'S CHEST. HE'S NERVOUS.

WINSTON: Now, you listen tae me. This is oor park. Ye're no' wanted here. Can ye no' underston that? We've done this fur wursels. There's nae need fur you tae annoy us anymair. Leave us alane.

THE TATTOOED MAN THINKS FOR A BEAT THEN GRABS THE STICK.

TATTOOED MAN:

Nup.

HE THROWS THE STICK OVER THE EDGE. THE DEVIL DOG LEAPS AFTER IT AND DISAPPEARS OVER THE EDGE OF THE BLOCK. THERE IS A LONG PAUSE AS WE CUT ROUND THE FACES. WE HEAR A SQUISH AND A MILD YELP.

6. DUG.

Back in the days when we were performing *Still Game* the play, we were invited to the theatre festival in Toronto. We went, it was well received but, more importantly, it was a fantastic holiday into the bargain for us and Paul Riley. Ever since then, we had been bouncing about ropey storylines where the outcome would be another trip to Toronto. We got our chance to lay the foundations for that trip with this episode. The only way we weren't getting to go was if they cancelled series three.

We are very fond of this episode as we get to explore the different relationships Jack and Victor have with their kids. Jack's daughter can't wait to see him, but Victor's son is too busy. This leads to Jack and Victor's very first fight.

We have also been partial to suggesting a budding romance between Winston and Isa and this episode seemed like the right place to do it. At the end of the second series, we had no intention of ever getting them together because Winston's short fuse with Isa's gossipy ways works so well and is one of the strongest dynamics of the show. To put them together would kill that off.

In the middle of this episode, Harry, Isa's estranged husband, played by Ronnie Letham, returns to attempt to woo his wife back. This leads to Winston pretending to court her and we think, the funniest scene in the run, where Winston and Isa are fully dressed and mock humping for Harry's benefit.

Ford and Greg

DUG.

1. EXT. HIGH FLATS. DAY.

THE RAIN IS LASHING DOWN.

VICTOR: Jesus Christ . . .

JACK: This is murder, intit? (looking at his watch) No' even nine a.m. and we're bastardin' wringin'.

VICTOR: Ma drawers are soakin'.

JACK: Ye shoulda went before ye came out.

VICTOR: Very funny, Jack.

JACK: That's Craiglang for ye. It's eternally winter here.

VICTOR: A bloody vortex.

JACK: That's it. I've made ma mind up. I'm gonnie kill masel'.

VICTOR: That's if ye dinnae droon first.

JACK: Huv ye never fancied gaun a big holiday?

VICTOR: What, Spain annat?

JACK: Naw – Hong Kong, America, a big adventure holiday.

VICTOR: Naw. It's a big enough adventure gaun over tae they shops ower there.

JACK: I've aye fancied it. Africa. Or doon the Nile. Or up the Congo. The Taj Mahal.

VICTOR: It's gettin' there's the problem. Fourteen hours on a plane at oor age
            – that would drive ye doolally.

JACK: Aye. The flight would do ye in. Aw crammed in there. Knees under
            the chin. Ye're waitin' on yer luggage at the other end. Blood clot.
            Thrombosis. Read aboot it. That's you, goodnight. And then they huv
            tae fly yer corpse home.

VICTOR: . . . and ye're doon below, in wi' aw the bananas and spiders. Deid.
            Some holiday, that.

JACK: Aye, right enough.

2. INT. LANDING. DAY.

JACK'S DOOR OPENS
FROM THE OUTSIDE.
JACK RUNS IN WITH
THE MESSAGES.

JACK: OOOH! Smashin'.
            That wis quick. Pick
            up that parcel, Victor.

VICTOR: What is it?

JACK: It's a tape fae ma Fiona.

VICTOR: Oh, aye?

JACK: Aye. I got it a couple of days ago but they don't play here, so I take
            them over tae Shug and he transfers them.

VICTOR: How don't they play?

JACK: 'Cause it's . . . Canadian – the tape's different.

VICTOR: Different how?

JACK: The actual tape that goes roon – it's different . . . tae oor tape. It's
            very technical.

VICTOR: Technical? Oh well, thank you.

JACK: Eh?

VICTOR: Christopher Hawkings. Thanking you.

JACK: Who, in the name of Christ, is Christopher Hawkings?

VICTOR: The brainy bastard. In the wheelchair. Wi' the voice.

JACK: Steven Hawkings.

VICTOR: Aye. Who did I say?

JACK: Christopher Hawkings.

VICTOR: Did I?

JACK: Anyway, what aboot him?

VICTOR: Nuthin'. De ye want a cup of tea?

JACK: Aye. You get the kettle on and I'll set up the video. (mumbling) Christopher Hawkings . . .

3. INT. NAVID'S SHOP. DAY.

ISA STANDS, MOP IN HAND, LOOKING OUT THE WINDOW.

ISA: It's lashin' doon the day. The sky's black.

NAVID: Here, Isa.

ISA: Aye.

NAVID: Did you watch *Stars in Their Eyes* on Saturday night?

ISA: Naw.

NAVID: Me and Meena never miss it – it's the highlight of the week for us, i'n't that right, Meena?

MEENA GRUNTS.

NAVID: Thanks fur joining in, ya boot. You should have seen the wee prick who won it. Frank Sinatra. Utter garbage. He was five feet. It was a joke, you know? Wee toattie Sinatra.

ISA: He must huv sounded like Sinatra if he won it?

NAVID: (tersely) Did he buggery. No one sounds like Sinatra. This guy was more like a gay Sinatra. A toattie wee midget gay Sinatra. Prick.

ISA: It's no' like me tae miss it. I generally watch it. I'd love tae be oan that. De ye know who I'd like tae be?

NAVID: Mama Cass?

ISA: (annoyed) Naw . . .

NAVID: Sorry. Who?

ISA: Patsy Cline.

NAVID: (completely deadpan) Patsy Cline? You'd be a good Patsy Cline. Gie's a wee blast.

ISA: Och, I don't like . . .

NAVID: Come on. The shop is empty.

ISA: (using the mop as a mic, Isa sings terribly) Craaaaaaaazy . . . I'm craaaaazy for feeling so lonely . . .

           NAVID LISTENS DEADPAN, WAITING UNTIL ISA STOPS SINGING.

NAVID: Tonight, Matthew, I'm going to be a bag of kittens drowning in the canal . . .

HARRY SLINKS INTO SHOT. HE IS SOAKING.

HARRY: I think ye're being a bit harsh there, Navid. (to Isa) I always thought you had a beautiful voice, sweetheart.

ISA: No, Harry, I'm no' even wanting tae speak tae ye.

HARRY: Now hear me out, darlin'.

ISA: Go away! I'm not interested in what ye've got to say!

HARRY: But, darlin'!

NAVID MARCHES ROUND THE COUNTER AND LIFTS HARRY BY THE COLLAR. HE CASUALLY EJECTS HIM FROM THE SHOP.

4. INT. JACK'S LIVING ROOM. DAY.

WE ARE LOOKING AT A VIDEO PLAYING ON THE TV. A PLEASANT LOOKING WOMAN, FORTY-ISH, SPLASHES AROUND IN A POOL.

FIONA: Hello, Dad!

JACK: Hello!

JACK CATCHES HIMSELF TALKING TO THE TAPE.

JACK: Look at her! She looks smashin'!

FIONA: We thought we'd send ye a wee home movie starring myself, Jack
            and Stephen!

            TWO BOYS, AGED ABOUT TEN AND TWELVE, COME INTO THE
            FRAME.

KIDS: Hi, Grampa!

JACK: Jeez-o. Listen tae their accents!

FIONA: . . . and, of course, the cameraman – Tony!

            THE CAMERA TURNS ON TO THE DAD WHO GRINS.

TONY: Hi, Jack!

            JACK AND VICTOR CHUCKLE AWAY.

FIONA: Oh! What's going on over here? Jack and Stephen are cooking
            burgers! How many burgers are you cooking?

KIDS: Five.

FIONA: Why five?

KIDS: Because we're cooking one for Grampa! Can you smell that,
            Grampa!

JACK: Looks smashin'.

KID: Take a bite!

JACK GETS UP AND
QUIETLY LEAVES
THE ROOM. HE
TAKES HIS HANKY
OUT THE POCKET
AND GOES INTO THE
KITCHEN. AFTER A
FEW MOMENTS,
VICTOR REALISES
HE IS WATCHING
THE TAPE HIMSELF. HE GETS UP AND FOLLOWS HIM OUT.

VICTOR: Jack. 'Smatter wi' ye?

JACK:	Nuthin' Victor. That tape caught me aff guard – seein' the size of the grandweans annat. Everytime I get wan of these tapes, it's the same – I sit doon aw excited and I end up depressed.

VICTOR: What aboot?

JACK: Missin' them, annat. I should huv bloody emigrated wi' them – when they asked me.

VICTOR: Aye . . . I sometimes wish I'd done that wi' ma John in Johannesburg. But ye cannae, can ye? Suppose they decide tae move again? That's you tae move again. And ye're just followin' them roon like a pup. That's nae life.

JACK: Naw. It isnae. Oor lives are here.

VICTOR: Aye.

JACK: Pish, eh?

VICTOR: Aye, it's pish. 'Mon, we'll get a pint.

5. INT. PUB. DAY.

WINSTON SITS, PEN IN HAND, WRITING ON A FOOTBALL CARD.
HE STARES AT A MECHANICAL DOG WHICH IS ON THE SHELF
ON THE GANTRY. IT HAS A BIT OF A4 ATTACHED TO IT WITH
THE FOLLOWING WRITTEN ON IT:
WIN ME!
GUESS MY NAME!

WINSTON: (reading the card) There's only a couple left.

BOABBY: Well, ye should huv got here earlier!

WINSTON: Shut up! Oliver. Doesnae look like an Oliver. Many huv you taken?

BOABBY: Three – Patch, Fido and Rex.

WINSTON: Ye fly bastard. Ye've swiped aw the guid dug names and left us wi' aw the shite. Christopher. Matthew. Richard? Richard the dug?

BOABBY: What can I say? I'm the landlord. It's ma caird.

HARRY:	Let's stop playing games, Isa. I love you.

ISA:	Well, I don't love you. I've met someone else.

HARRY:	What! Who?

ISA:	None of your business. Now leave me alone!

SHE THROWS THE CRUMPLED TENNER AT HIM AND HEADS INTO THE CLANSMAN.

7. INT. CLANSMAN. DAY.

ISA BURSTS IN. SHE'S PALE AND SHAKEN.

ISA:	Sherry, Boabby.

VICTOR:	Isa, are ye awright, hen?

ISA:	Naw. Harry's back.

WINSTON:	What!?

ISA:	And that's not all! I've telt him I've got a fella!

JACK:	Eh?

HARRY ENTERS THE BAR. THE BAR IS SUSPICIOUS OF HARRY.

BOABBY:	(While watching Harry) There's yer sherry, darlin'.

HARRY:	Lager please, Boabby. Allow me, sweetheart.

WINSTON:	I'll be payin' fur Isa's, Harry.

WINSTON STEPS FORWARD AND PLACES AN AWKWARD ARM
AROUND ISA'S WAIST. SHE CUDDLES INTO HIM.

HARRY: (disbelieving) You're the new fella?

WINSTON: That's right. Crackin' wummin. Bit of a gabshite but generally lovely.

THERE'S A SOUR ATMOSPHERE. JACK PIPES UP IN AN
ATTEMPT TO ALLEVIATE IT.

JACK: Right. Who's won the dug?

WINSTON: (mumbling) Looks like I huv . . .

JACK: Eh?

WINSTON: Nuthin'.

JACK: Boabby, scrape it aff.

BOBBY: (ringing the bell) Attention everybody!

WE GET A SHOT OF THE PUB. IT'S HALF EMPTY AND NOBODY
GIVES A TOSS.

BOBBY: The winner of the name-the-dug competition is . . . Matthew.

VICTOR: Smashin'. Gie's ma
            dug. 'Mere, Matthew.

            HE TURNS IT ON.
            MATTHEW TILTS HIS
            HEAD AND HIS EYES
            LIGHT UP.

VICTOR: Is that it?

BOABBY: Ye've gottae train it.
            Gie' it commands.

JACK: Matthew (pointing an
            aggressive finger at
            Harry) – bite his
            baws!!!

8. INT. JACK'S FLAT. NIGHT.

JACK SITS WATCHING FIONA'S VIDEO. IT COMES TO AN END. HE TURNS IT OFF AND SITS FOR A MOMENT. HE REACHES FOR HIS PHONE AND DIALS.

JACK: Oh, ye're in! I was just gonnie leave a message. What time is it there? Hof eight here . . . Aye, I got it. I'm just after watchin' it. Fantastic. That wis guid of ye. Jack and Stephen look a right honfae! Smashin' boys, but. Huv you lost weight? Ye're no' as broad in the arse as ye used tae be! Eh? He-he-he. I'm only windin' ye up. I'm fine. Aye, never been rosier. Victor's fine, aye. He's got a new dug. No' a real dug. A silver dug. Never mind. Eh? Eh? Awf, I dunno about that. When, were you thinkin'? Owf, no. No, no, I know. Eh . . . Can I think aboot it? I dunno – tomorrow? Right. Speak tae ye then. Love you too, darlin'.

HE PUTS PHONE DOWN AND SITS IN SILENCE.

JACK: Canada . . .

9. INT. NAVID'S SHOP. MORNING.

NAVID STANDS AT THE COUNTER. HARRY ENTERS.

NAVID: Oh-oh. Here we go.

HARRY: Mornin', Navid.

NAVID: Morning, Harry. What can I get you?

HARRY: Twenty Benson and Hedges. I hear ma Isa's hooked up wi' Winston.

NAVID: How do you mean 'hooked up'?

HARRY: Gaun oot – together.

NAVID COLLAPSES IN LAUGHTER.

NAVID: Winston and Isa? That's a belter, right enough. Winston hates Isa! Only the other day they were in here, she was yakking, yakyakyakyakyak. And he said, 'If I had a gun, I would shoot you in the face Isa!' Naw, Harry. Check your Y-fronts. Somebody is pulling your pisser. Twenty Benson and Hedges.

HARRY: Ye couldnae possibly let me huv . . .

NAVID: No, no, no, no, no, no, no, no, no. Sorry did I say no there? I meant to say NO!

HARRY: C'mon, Navid. Isa'll gie ye the money back.

NAVID: Jesus. Tapping Isa in her absence. Unbelievable. Don't get me wrong, Harry. There are many people on ma tick list. But there are two names that will never appear on it. You . . . and Osama Bin Laden.

HARRY: It's only twenty fags, Navid.

NAVID: (turning to show Harry the back of his head) Do you see buttons, a zipper, Velcro or any other fastening device? No. Sling yer hook ye panhandling bastard.

           HARRY LEAVES THE SHOP.

10. EXT. NAVID'S SHOP. DAY.

           ISA IS WALKING WITH WINSTON. WE CUT OVER TO THEM.

WINSTON: How long huv I tae dae awe this walkin' aboot with ye? I'm choking fur a pint.

ISA: Lager? At this time of the day?

WINSTON: Jesus. There we've only been gaun oot two minutes and ye're naggin' me already! I want a divorce!

ISA: It's just fur a couple of days, Winston – till Harry gets the message.

               ERIC WALKS BY DOING THE INTERNATIONAL SIGN FOR
               SHAGGING BEHIND ISA'S BACK.

WINSTON: It's the message everybody else is gettin' I'm worried about.

               ISA SPOTS HARRY COMING OUT OF NAVID'S.

ISA: Oh, God. There he is. Gie's yer airm.

WINSTON: Naw, naw. That's no' part of the deal. Nae touchin'.

ISA: Winston, please!

WINSTON: (reluctantly) Ri-i-ight.

               THEY CROSS THE ROAD AND STAND OUTSIDE NAVID'S.

ISA: Harry.

HARRY: Isa. Winston.

WINSTON: Harry.

ISA: (awkwardly) Thanks fur walking me to ma work, pumpkin.

WINSTON: Pumpkin? Nae
               problem, Pumpkin.

ISA: Now away and get
               yersel' a pint.

WINSTON: A pint? That's a rare
               idea. (To Harry) It's
               no' many . . .
               girlfriends that let
               you go get a pint.

HARRY: No, it is not.

ISA: Don't make anythin' for the night's tea. I'll bring in yer favourite.

WINSTON: OOOH, ma favourite! (pausing) Which is a sausage supp~ .

ISA: (rolling her eyes for Harry's benefit) I know that!

WINSTON: I know you know that.

ISA: Well, then. Goodbye.

                ISA PLANTS A KISS FULL ON WINSTON'S MOUTH.

WINSTON: Jesus! Eh . . . that wis smashin'! Yum, yum.

                ISA GOES INTO THE SHOP. WINSTON SAUNTERS AWAY
                STIFFLY. HARRY EYES HIM SUSPICIOUSLY.

11. EXT. PARK. DAY.

                VICTOR SITS ON THE BENCH, READING A MANUAL. MATTHEW
                SITS AT HIS FEET, MOTIONLESS

VICTOR: Wag yer wee tail.
                Naw? OK, then . . .
                bark. Nuthin'. Are ye
                hungry? Listen tae me
                – are ye hungry?
                (referring to a book)
                Clap your hands and
                the dug will flip.

                VICTOR CLAPS.

VICTOR: Flip. Flip.

                JACK APPEARS. HE SITS NEXT TO VICTOR.

JACK: Hey-ho.

VICTOR: Hello, Jack.

JACK: How ye getting on wi the dug?

VICTOR: No' very well. I think he's depressed.

JACK: Depressed? Yer wee plastic dug's depressed? Well there ye go.
                Mebbe it's constipatit. Mebbe it's needin tae lift its wee tail and shite
                oot a wee plastic jobbie then it'll no' be fed up, ya hofwit.

JACK: Are ye phonin'?

VICTOR: Eh? Naw.

JACK: Get 'im phoned. Go on. Tell him ye want tae go over at end of next
           week.

VICTOR: I know what he's gonnie say.

JACK: What's he gonnie say?

VICTOR: He'll say naw.

JACK: Ye don't know that fur sure.

VICTOR: Aye, I dae. He's aye lettin' me doon. He's no' like your Fiona. He'll
           say naw.

JACK: Phone 'im. I'll put the kettle on. Go on. Just tell 'im ye're wantin' a
           wee hoaliday.

           RELUCTANTLY, VICTOR STEPS UP TO THE PHONE. HE DIALS.

VICTOR: . . . John. It's yer da. How's it gaun, son? Aye, guid. Eh? Naw, nothin'.
           I wis just gonnie say, Jack's gaun tae Canada so I wis thinking . . .
           No, no . . . I wis gonnie come and see youse rather than sit aboot
           here on ma arse for a fortnight while Jack's away. End of next week.
           I know it is soon – bit last minute. But, eh . . . eh? Well, what aboot
           the followin' week then? . . . Oh, are ye? Ach, well. Not at all – I
           thought it might be tight for yis. Well, when would be best . . . tae
           come over? Aye, well,
           I'll phone ye . . . Naw,
           naw, I know that. Oh!
           There's the doorbell –
           I'll need tae go. Gie
           ma best to the boy,
           annat. See ye now.

           VICTOR REPLACES
           THE PHONE AND
           SITS DOWN.

JACK: How did that go?

VICTOR: How did that go? Lousy. That's how it went, ya stupid basta.

JACK: How am I a stupid bastard?

VICTOR: I telt ye he'd say no but you're at me – 'Phone 'im, phone 'im!' Well,
            there ye are. Happy noo? I've phoned him and he's chased me.

JACK: Mebbe he's busy, Victor.

VICTOR: Aye, so he is. I could hear the bloody wheels turnin', tryin' tae think
            up a reason tae no' huv me there.

JACK: What wis the reason?

VICTOR: A convention in bloody Cape Town. Lotta shite.

JACK: Well, that's that then. Just come wi' me. Ma Fiona said . . .

VICTOR: Your Fiona. Your Fiona. That's right, I forgot. Your Fiona's an angel.
            'Come on over, Dad, and bring as many of yer sad old pals as ye
            can squeeze on tae the plane.'

JACK: Now wait a minute . . .

VICTOR: You wait a minute. I'm
            no' a charity case. I
            wis daein' fine till you
            brought aw this up in
            the first place.

JACK: Now look, Victor . . .

VICTOR: Naw. I know fine how
            much ma boy isnae
            interested in me and you, ya bastard, railroadin' me intae bein'
            reminded of the fact!

JACK: I wis just thinkin' ye could get a hoaliday.

            I will be gettin' a hoaliday – a hoaliday fae you!

            fine.

            GOES OUT AND SLAMS THE DOOR. VICTOR IS LEFT ALONE.
            ELLS SOMETHING. CUT TO SEE THAT MATTHEW HAS
            WLED ON TO THE GRATE OF THE BAR FIRE AND IS SMOKING.

VICTOR: Matthew!

MONTAGE SEQUENCE FOLLOWS. WINSTON IS BEING
DRAGGED VARIOUS PLACES BY ISA. CUT TO THE PUB WHERE
WINSTON IS OFFERING HIS HANDS TO HOLD WOOL WHILE ISA
KNITS AND CHATS TO TWO FEMALE PALS. HARRY IS LOOKING
ON. WE SEE THEM IN A CAFÉ. ISA IS PUTTING MORE SUGAR
IN WINSTON'S TEA. HE IS TRYING TO STOP HER. HARRY
WATCHES ON. CUT TO THE CINEMA WHERE WINSTON IS
TRYING TO WATCH WHILE ISA TALKS INCESSANTLY. THREE
ROWS BACK SITS HARRY. CUT TO WINSTON ABOUT TO HEAD
INTO THE BOOKIE'S AND ISA PULLS HIM TOWARDS THE
BINGO. CUT TO WINSTON STANDING HAVING A PINT. ISA

STORMS IN AND
PLONKS HIS DINNER
DOWN IN FRONT OF
HIM. SHE TWEEKS
HIS CHEEK AND
SHAKES A FRIENDLY
FIST AT HIM. HARRY
AND THE REST OF
THE PUB GOES INTO
A KINK.

13. EXT. STREET. NIGHT.

JACK CUTS A LONELY FIGURE WALKING ALONG AND
ENTERING THE CLANSMAN.

14. INT. PUB. NIGHT.

JACK ENTERS. HE CLOCKS VICTOR READING HIS PAPER AT
THE END OF THE BAR. THEY EXCHANGE LOOKS.
APPROACHES THE BAR. WINSTON STANDS AT F
IS LIKE FIZZ, HE IS EATING HIS DINNER.

JACK: Well, you couldnae huv ordered that here —

WINSTON: Don't ask.

JACK: How ye gettin' on wi' the Harry thing? Is he s

WINSTON: Like a shadow. Bastard. He's in there playin' pool the noo. He doesnae believe us. He's waitin' fur us tae slip up.

JACK: How long's that?

WINSTON: A week. It's no' that. Every night I've tae walk her hame, past ma ain hoose, up tae hers and I've tae sit another hoor tae make sure creepy-breeks isnae hangin' aboot outside! I'm demented wi' it. What's the deal wi' you and Victor? Still no' talkin'?

JACK: Naw. And I'm no' wantin' it tae drag on an' all 'cause I'm away in the mornin'.

VICTOR SIDLES OVER AND PUTS AN EMPTY PINT GLASS DOWN.

VICTOR: Pint of lager, Boabby.

WINSTON GIVES JACK A NOD AS IF TO SAY, 'HERE'S YOUR CHANCE.'

JACK: I'll get that.

VICTOR: Thanks for that, Jack. Away in the mornin' then?

JACK: Aye. I wish you were comin' wi' me.

VICTOR: Aye, well, mebbe the next time.

JACK: Look, I didnae mean tae force ye intae phonin' your John.

VICTOR: Jack, ma John isnae interested in me and I shouldnae be takin' that oot on you.

VICTOR:

tthew anyway?

JACK: Well,

arsehole?! Lost 'im fur two hours the other day. Where Guid. him? In the oven.

JACK G gas 'issel'?

E SM

RAV e you no' takin' a pint?

JACK:　　　I wisnae gonnie. I've packin' tae dae.

VICTOR:　　'Mon. Quick pint tae see ye aff.

JACK:　　　Aye.

WINSTON:　Am I no' tae get one?

BOABBY:　Naw. Too many pints affects yer performance!

　　　　　　BOABBY DOES A HUMPING GESTURE.

ISA:　　　　Right enough, Boabby! C'mon you! Ye're nae use tae me aw floppy!

　　　　　　THE PUB FALLS ABOUT. WINSTON FOLLOWS ISA OUT, HIS
　　　　　　HEART ROASTED.

15. INT. ISA'S FLAT. NIGHT.

　　　　　　WINSTON SITS HOLDING A BEER CAN AND EATING A
　　　　　　SANDWICH.

WINSTON:　Floppy? Where the hell did that come fae?

ISA:　　　　I'm sorry, Winston! It was oot before I realised! It wis Harry sittin'
　　　　　　there. He wis makin' me aw jumpy.

WINSTON:　Well, look at it this
　　　　　　way, Isa. He must huv
　　　　　　the message by noo.
　　　　　　So I'm aff the hook
　　　　　　and we can get back
　　　　　　tae wur ain thing.

ISA:　　　　It husnae been that
　　　　　　bad, has it?

　　　　　　WINSTON LOOKS AT HER.

ISA:　　　　I mean, I've always got a drink in fur y�?
　　　　　　sandwiches and cakes! I've never seen a t�
　　　　　　And we've hud a guid laugh tae!

WINSTON:　When?

ISA: The other night, we
              were watching the
              news and Jackie Bird
              came on and I said,
              'De ye think, when
              her and her man are
              startin' tae make
              love, she shouts,
              "THIS JUST IN!"'

WINSTON SPLUTTERS HIS BEER AND STARTS TO LAUGH.
THEY BOTH CHUCKLE. AS IT DIES DOWN, THEY SHARE A WEE
MOMENT. IT IS INTERRUPTED BY THE DOORBELL.

ISA: Oh, God. Who will that be? It might be Harry!

WINSTON: Calm doon. 'Mon.

              WINSTON GOES UP TO THE PEEPHOLE. WE SEE HIS POV.
              HARRY STANDS ON THE LANDING.

WINSTON: It is an' aw . . .

ISA: What'll we dae?

WINSTON: Just ignore it. He'll go away!

              THERE'S A JANGLING IN THE LOCK.

ISA: I forgot! He must still huv keys!

WINSTON: Jesus! Right.

              WINSTON BUNDLES ISA INTO THE BEDROOM JUST AS THE
              DOOR OPENS.

              Isa? Isaaaa? Isa, sweetheart?

              HARRY WALKS
              THROUGH THE FLAT.
              THE TELLY IS ON. HE
              ⬚⬚ ⬚ ⬚ CAN OF
              ⬚⬚⬚ HALF-
              ⬚ ⬚NDWICH.
              ⬚ ⬚⬚US. HE
              ⬚⬚WN THE

HALL. HE PUTS HIS HAND ON THE BEDROOM DOOR AND
SLOWLY OPENS IT. HE SEES THE DUVET GOING UP AND
DOWN IN THE MANNER OF HUMPING. FROM BENEATH THE
DUVET WE HEAR:

WINSTON: 'Ere ye are, hen! Get that slung up ye! 'Ere's hee-haw floppy here!

HARRY CASUALLY WALKS UP AND PULLS THE DUVET BACK.
WINSTON IS PRETENDING TO HUMP ISA. THEY ARE BOTH
FULLY CLOTHED. THEY REALISE THEY HAVE BEEN RUMBLED

AND GRADUALLY
GRIND TO A HALT.
WINSTON
AWKWARDLY CLIMBS
OFF ISA AND SITS
UP. ISA SITS UP TOO.
THEY LOOK
EMBARRASSED AND
GUILTY.

16. INT. ISA'S LIVING ROOM. NIGHT.

HARRY AND ISA SIT AT OPPOSITE ENDS OF THE TABLE.
WINSTON PLONKS TWO CUPS OF TEA DOWN AND MAKES
HIMSELF SCARCE.

HARRY: I knew fae the beginning. Nae offence, Winston but ye're hardly a
            match.

WINSTON EYES HIM. HE RETURNS TO WATCHING THE TELLY.

ISA: Harry, ye've seen the lengths I've went tae get the message across
            tae ye.

HARRY: I know, darlin'.

ISA: It's finished. Can ye
            no' just accept it?

HARRY SIGHS AND
PLACES HIS KEYS
ON THE TABLE. HE
SMILES AT HER.

HARRY: I'll see masel' oot. Goodbye, Isa.

ISA: Goodbye, Harry.

HARRY: Cheerio, Winston.

WINSTON: (without turning) Cheerio, Harry.

              HARRY LEAVES.

17. INT. PLANE SITTING ON THE TARMAC. DAY

              JACK SITS IN THE MIDDLE SEAT. A YOUNG MAN SITS DOWN IN
              THE AISLE SEAT.

MAN: How ye daein'?

JACK: Aye, guid.

MAN: Looking forward to the flight?

JACK: Aye, well, I'll wait and see who's sittin' here first. Ye aye get an
              arsehole on these long hauls, dint ye?

              THEY BOTH SHARE A CHUCKLE.

MAN: Aye, ye dae . . .

              AN OLD FELLA
              UPROOTS THEM TO
              SIT DOWN. WHAT
              FOLLOWS IS A PISS-
              POOR COMEDY
              MONOLOGUE
              DURING WHICH JACK
              HIS HEAD IN
              S.

              The windae seat! I've got a weak bladder an' aw. I'll be
              on like a bloody yoyo! New York, eh? Cannae wait! I'm
              ' Toronto, eh? Jeez-o. (cracking open a bottle of duty-
              no' supposed tae drink yer ain but I'm no' waitin' an
              y crack open the bevvy trolley! Is there a film? But
              ayin fur heidphones – (for the benefit of a passing

stewardess) I say, I'll no' be payin fur headphones. Saw the Captain on the way in – pished as a fart he was, pished as a fart. Dunno how we'll fare wi' that bastard. (slapping Jack's shoulder) I'm only takin' the piss, son. (sings) COME FLY WI' ME, FLOAT ON TO PERU . . .

VICTOR: (from the aisle) I think you're in ma seat, pal – fourteen D.

OLD FELLA: Sorry aboot that, governor. (looking out the window) Look at that! The people look like ants! Oh, they are ants! We huvnae takin' aff yet! Right oot ma road.

THE OLD FELLA STRUGGLES OUT. VICTOR STRUGGLES IN.

JACK: Ye fly bastard!

VICTOR: I booked it yesterday. I'm no' sittin' on ma arse for a fortnight while your havin' a guid time.

JACK: He-he-he.

THEY LAUGH AND BURST INTO 'COME FLY WITH ME'.

CLOSING MUSIC AND CREDITS, THEN:

A PICTURE OF DOMESTICITY. ISA AND WINSTON ARE ENJOYING A GOOD LAUGH AS THEY SIT BY THE FIRE. IN FRONT OF THEM, MATTHEW THE DOG WAGS HIS TAIL, BARKS AND DOES REPEATED BACK FLIPS.

ISA: Happy wee thing, eh?

WINSTON: Aye.